# FORTY FAVORITE CHILDREN'S STORIES

*By*
*Lawrence Maxwell*

*Illustrations by*
*Joyce Kimbel*

TEACH Services, Inc.
PUBLISHING
www.TEACHServices.com • (800) 367-1844

ISBN-13: 978-1-57258-573-7 (Paperback)
Library of Congress Control Number: 2008937259

Originally published under the names
*What Stopped the Music* and *Outnumbered*

# CONTENTS

# READ THIS FIRST

What would happen if a person took the Bible seriously and tried to live up to everything it says?

This book is about people—mostly teen-agers—who tried to find out.

Just to name a few of them, you'll read about Nancy, who asked God to help her when she couldn't do her homework.

You'll read about Dick, who loved to smoke, but who dared to let someone pray that he would stop.

And you will find Lois, whose family experimented with paying tithe when their farm was about to be detroyed by grasshoppers.

You will probably feel that the last two chapters are the best. In them you will read what God has promised to do for everyone who lives every day the way the Bible says we should.

Some of the stories may seem hard to believe, but they are all true, even "What Stopped the Music." I know both John and his mother well, and it was John's mother who told me what happened to that record player. "Mike's Mystery" I learned firsthand, standing outside on the church steps one night, listening to Mike himself reliving the experience. All the stories are true accounts of real people who took God at His word.

When you've finished the book, you may want to conduct a few experiments for yourself. Go ahead. God says, "Prove Me." So take Him at His word. Pray for something you want very much. Or start paying tithe. Or ask God to give you victory over some bad habit. Be specific. And don't rush God. Give Him time to work. He will do something very wonderful for you.

## WHAT STOPPED THE MUSIC

John dusted the little Bible and set it back on top of the pile of magazines above his bookcase. Then he dusted his record player.

He had had this player for a year now. He remembered when he got it. Mother had been quite disturbed. She asked him what kind of records he intended to play on it, and he told her. Most of them were the current hits, and she said she did not like them. But he had played them anyway.

One day she said to him, "John, it is your privilege and mine to choose what goes into our minds. We can store them full of rubbish if we wish. Or we can fill them with the best and the finest. This is true of the books and magazines we read, the kind of TV programs we watch, and the music we listen to. You know what I'd like to have you choose, don't you, Son?"

Mother got up then and went to another room and left John thinking. He wished his mother wouldn't put things the way she did. But he respected her, so he picked out all the records she didn't like and threw them away.

All of that was a year ago.

Now it was the afternoon when our story began. Something snapped inside John that day. Everybody at school had been singing a new song. They said the disc jockeys were calling it the top of the hit parade. Really sweeping the country, they said. And John hadn't even heard it before he reached school that morning.

He looked around. He was alone in the house. Dad was at work, of course. Mother and Sister were shopping.

He flung the dustcloth on his bed, glanced at himself in the mirror, and dashed for the door.

With a strange feeling of excitement, he rushed up the street to a record store.

Dozens of records of the song he wanted were on display in the store windows. Quite obviously, it was all the rage. He pointed to one; the clerk wrapped it up. He paid for it and headed home.

He hadn't been gone more than twenty minutes. Mother was still out. He put the record on the player, and immediately the house was filled with a weird, wild beat.

John tingled from head to toe. No wonder everyone was so excited about this new tune!

Suddenly the music stopped. There was a cry from John—and the house fell silent.

When Mother came in an hour or so later, John led her to his bedroom and pointed to the record player. The pickup arm that held the needle was broken in two.

"What happened?" Mother asked.

"That's just what I want to tell you," John said. "You see, I got this record today."

Mother read the title and her face grew sad.

John said, "I'm sorry, Mom. But wait till I've finished. You see, I put this record on and began to play it. Now, my Bible was sitting on top of this pile of magazines on the bookcase, here."

He showed her exactly where the Bible had been.

"Well, when the record got about halfway through, the Bible fell down off the bookcase onto the needle arm and broke it. Yet look, Mom, the arm is made of plastic and is half an inch thick, and the Bible is only a little one.

"I can't figure out what made it slide off the book-case just when it did. Unless—Do you suppose maybe God made it happen because He was trying to teach me a lesson?"

Mother's voice was serious. "Yes, Son, I think maybe He did. I never have believed He liked that kind of music."

The record player has been fixed. John's mother told me the other day that John uses it only for the best and finest music. He has not played another "wild" record on it from that day to this.

## MIKE'S MYSTERY

A snowstorm was blowing when Mike got out of school that afternoon. He jerked his collar up around his neck and dashed for the bus.

It was amazing how quiet everything sounded, and how slowly the traffic was moving. All the buses were late, but Mike didn't realize that. He saw one that looked like his and climbed aboard.

After traveling several miles he glanced out the window and noticed that the streets didn't look right. He was on the wrong bus!

He would have to get another bus and go back. Did he have enough money for the fare?

He felt in his pocket. Three nickels—fifteen cents. The bus fare back to the school would be ten cents. The fare from school to home would be another ten cents. He didn't have enough!

Then another idea occurred to him, and he relaxed. He could get off the bus at the next stop and phone home and ask Mother to come to the school for him. That would cost a nickel—for this happened when phone calls cost only five cents. The bus fare back to the school would be ten cents. The total would be fifteen cents, exactly what he had.

He got off at the next stop and walked to a drugstore on the corner. The building was crowded with people, mostly children from school trying to keep warm till their buses came. He pushed his way in. The place had a damp, close smell about it.

There was a public phone on the far wall.

Mike put a nickel in and dialed. Really, considering the problem, things were working out remarkably well.

He heard the phone ring once on the other end. Then the line went dead.

Mike had never known a phone to act that way before. He hung up and looked for the nickel to come back, but it didn't.

Better try again.

He put in another nickel and dialed. The phone rang once—and died.

He put in another nickel and dialed a third time. Again the phone rang once and died.

Mike suddenly realized that his money was gone. He was alone, miles from home, with night coming on and a storm blowing, and no one to help him.

Unless Jesus would.

Mike was sure Jesus could. The Bible told of a thousand wonderful things Jesus did in days gone by. But would He? Would Jesus help a boy find a dime to get home with—in these days?

Mike had it figured out now that a dime would be enough. Ten cents would pay the bus fare back to school, and he had a friend who lived near the bus stop who had a phone he could use to call home.

He closed his eyes in the middle of that crowded store and prayed. "Dear Jesus, please help me get a dime. I'm here all alone by myself, and there isn't anyone else to help me but You."

He opened his eyes, and a very wonderful thing happened. A man walked into the store and looked all the boys over carefully. Then he said, "You, boy. Would you like to earn a dime?"

He was pointing at Mike!

"Yes, SIR!" Mike said.

"Then come with me," the man said. "My car's stalled outside and I need someone to help me push it. Will you do that?"

Mike pushed, the car started, and the man paid him the dime.

Mike was soon on his way home, sitting in the bus, wondering at the marvelous mystery of it all. Why did the man's car stall when it did? Why did the man look the boys over so carefully? Why did he choose him? Why did he offer to pay exactly a dime?

"Dear Jesus," Mike whispered. "Now I know You really do love me, not just because of what the Bible says, but because of what You have done for me today. Thank You so much."

# IMMOVABLE ELEPHANT

This story comes from the days when the British ruled India. It was first printed in the London *Times*.

It happened during a war in India. The army of one of the provinces in central India was fighting the army of another province.

The peshwa (the chief officer of one of these provinces) had given the flag to his most trusted elephant driver and ordered him to keep it flying. The elephant driver, or mahout as he was called, fastened the flag to his elephant where everyone could see it.

At first the battle went in favor of the peshwa. Then his army ran into difficulties. The mahout ordered his elephant to halt—and a moment later the mahout was killed.

Now things really went bad for the peshwa's army. Many of his soldiers were sure there was no hope and that they had better escape while they were still alive.

Then for a moment the smoke cleared from the battlefield. The fearful soldiers saw that their flag was still flying above the elephant and that it had not retreated so much as one foot.

If the flag was still flying, there was still a chance to win! The men took new courage and redoubled their efforts. The battle swept past the immovable elephant in the opposite direction and left him standing like a mountain among the bodies of the slain! Sure that their case was hopeless, the enemy broke and ran.

The peshwa's victorious soldiers gathered round their elephant and showered praise upon him. Then, because it was time to go home, one of the other mahouts mounted to the elephant's shoulders and ordered him to follow the rest of the elephants, which were leaving the battlefield. But the flag-bearing elephant would not move.

His master had told him to stay where he was and to carry the flag. And until his master changed the order he would stay where he was, and fly the flag.

Other mahouts tried, but to no avail. Three days went by. The elephant still stood in the same place. Then someone remembered that the mahout had a son, a little boy whom the mahout had occasionally put in charge of the elephant. They sent for him, though the boy lived a hundred miles away.

When he came, the elephant recognized the voice of his master's son. With the broken trappings of battle clanging against his sides, he followed the boy home.

Every once in a while we find ourselves in the middle of a group of young people who are being swept along into various kinds of sin. Next time this happens to you, remember the immovable elephant. If you will stand where you are and keep the flag flying for the King of kings, some of your friends will see your example and will take courage again. They will resist the devil till they win the victory.

## SISTER CLANCY

Sister Clancy was an elderly Irish woman who lived by herself in New York. Everyone called her Sister Clancy, so we will, too.

She heard there were going to be some meetings about the Bible in a large auditorium near to the one small room that she called home. She loved the Bible, so she decided to go.

She knew that the preacher's name was Mr. Haynes. She didn't notice what church he belonged to. She didn't think that mattered.

She enjoyed the first meeting ever so much. Night after night she returned, drinking in every word. In fact, each new sermon seemed more interesting and helpful than anything she had heard before.

She took a piece of paper and a pencil with her and carefully wrote down the texts the preacher referred to. Later, at home, she would look them all up in her Bible and check them. She didn't want this preacher putting anything over on her. So far, everything checked out with the Bible.

One night the preacher talked about tithing. He read from the third chapter of Malachi, "Will a man rob God? Yet ye have robbed Me. But ye say, Where-in have we robbed Thee? In tithes and offerings."

The preacher paused. "You see," he said to the congregation, "the Israelites thought they were just about perfect. But God called them robbers. When the people asked the prophet what He meant by that, Malachi told them they were robbing God because they were not giving Him their tithes and offerings."

Mr. Haynes went on. "Listen to what God said the people should do. You'll find it in the tenth verse: 'Bring ye all the tithes into the storehouse,...and prove Me now herewith, saith the Lord of hosts, if I will not open you the windows of heaven, and pour you out a blessing, that there shall not be room enough to receive it.' "

Sister Clancy sat up and took notice. What was this tithe thing the preacher was talking about? She had never paid any in all her life. What was tithe?

As if he knew her thoughts, the preacher said, "God tells us exactly what the tithe is, in Leviticus 27:32: 'And concerning the tithe,...the tenth shall be holy unto the Lord.' This means"—Mr. Haynes smiled pleasantly over his congregation—"that one tenth of our income belongs to the Lord, and we should give it to Him as tithe."

This was news to Sister Clancy. Was she really a robber? She certainly didn't mean to be. She felt she ought to ask the preacher about it.

When the meeting was over, she shook the preacher's hand at the door. "Mr. Haynes," she said, "I have a question. Now, I want you to listen carefully to everything I have to say before you answer.

"This is the way it is with me, Mr. Haynes. I am a widow. I have no money coming in except for six dollars that a nephew sends me every week. I live in just one room, and my rent is $4.50 a week. That leaves me $1.50 to buy all my food and clothes—everything.

"Now, if I pay tithe, as you said tonight, that would be one tenth of $6.00, which is 60 cents. And that would mean that I would have sixty cents less than $1.50—just 90 cents to live on all week. Tell me, pastor, does God expect me to pay tithe under these circumstances?"

Mr. Haynes wanted to say to her, "God can get along without your tithe, Sister Clancy. You don't have to pay any." But then he thought, Who am I to tell someone she doesn't need to obey God?

So he said instead, "Sister Clancy, God asks you to pay tithe, and He will bless you if you do."

"Very well," Sister Clancy answered. "I have trusted Him all my life, and He has never failed me."

A week later, as he stood at the door shaking hands with the people who had come to the meeting, the preacher felt Sister Clancy place something in his right hand. He glanced down to see what it was.

Sixty cents!

The next week Sister Clancy did the same. Pastor Haynes had just time to whisper, "Is everything all right, sister?"

She beamed. "It's wonderful!"

There was a little more time to talk another night, and this time Sister Clancy exclaimed, "I've never had it so good, pastor! Folks keep bringing me things—bread and fruit and other things. They never did before. Why I'm living a whole lot better on my 90 cents than ever I did on $1.50!"

Three or four more weeks went by. Pastor Haynes was studying in his office. It was evening, and the streets were dark.

There was a loud knocking on his door, and in walked Sister Clancy. She strutted importantly, back and forth, in front of his desk.

"Ye must respect me now, that ye must," she said, and there was a twinkle in her eye. "I'm a wealthy woman now, I am. Bless the Lord, He's been good to me."

"Now, come, come, Sister Clancy. Won't you please sit down and tell me what has happened?"

"Ah, I'm rich, I tell ye. Praise the Lord! You said He'd bless me, and I believed it, and He has. But I never expected He'd do it this way, or give me so much."

"Please, Sister Clancy. This sounds wonderful, and I want to hear all about it. Won't you please sit down and explain yourself?" Mr. Haynes walked around and slid a chair toward the elderly lady. "Here, Sister Clancy, you could sit on this."

At last the good woman calmed down. Mr. Haynes repeated his request. "Tell me what has happened."

"Well," she began, "I've been paying tithe, as you know, sixty cents a week. And you said the Lord would bless me if I did. Do you remember that nephew that has been sending me six dollars a week? God bless him! Listen to this. He sent me a letter. Here, I've got it with me. I'll read it to you."

She searched in her handbag for a moment. "Yes, here it is. Listen. 'Dear Aunty: For a long time I've been wanting to send you more than six dollars every week, but I couldn't. Now at last I've had a raise. So here is ten dollars, and from now on, it will be ten dollars that I will send you every week.'"

She looked up, and Mr. Haynes saw tears of gratitude in her eyes.

"Don't you see, pastor? My tithe goes up to $1.00, but my rent remains the same, $4.50. That's $5.50 for rent and tithe, and I have $4.50 left for myself—three times as much as the $1.50 I had before I began paying tithe.

"Oh, pastor, I just don't know what I'm going to do with all my money! The Lord has been good to me, so very, very good. I'm so glad you preached about tithe that night."

God's promise to bless people who pay tithe is not just for elderly ladies. It is for everyone—boys and girls and teenagers too.

If you want a really interesting experience, start paying tithe. When you earn some money, give one tenth of it as tithe to God. You could hand it to your pastor next time you go to church. Tell him it is tithe. Do this regularly, with all the money you earn.

Then watch and see what God will do for you when He opens the windows of heaven and sends you a blessing so big you won't have room enough for it.

## GOD CHASED THE GRASSHOPPERS!

That story about Sister Clancy, and how God blessed her when she paid tithe, makes me think of the wonderful blessing God sent to Lois and her family when they began to pay tithe. It really was a miracle. I learned about it from a man who knew the facts.

Grasshoppers!

They were everywhere. In the field, in the garden, on the window screens. Chewing up all the crops.

But the grasshoppers that were trying to get into Lois's garden were completely frustrated! Right in front of them lay the most luscious vegetables their eyes had ever gazed on, but for some inexplicable reason they couldn't get into the garden to eat them!

Yet they couldn't see anything stopping them. And no one else could either! That was what made the whole thing so remarkable.

The chain of events leading to this amazing experience began in the fall, some years ago, near Chain Lakes in Martin County, Minnesota.

Lois was walking around the family farm when, in the middle of the vegetable patch, she suddenly stood stock still. A wave of discouragement almost made her weep.

Grasshoppers were everywhere—even walking over her shoes, climbing up her legs, flying in her face!

She knew, too, that the ground was full of grasshopper eggs. For miles around it was the same way. The county had offered a bounty for all grasshoppers that were brought to the county building. Thousands upon thousands of grasshoppers had been caught and turned in, but what were they among so many?

And what would happen next spring, when the eggs hatched?

Lois walked sadly back to the house. Dad had grown old and feeble. He couldn't run the farm anymore. And Mother wasn't strong enough to do much, either. Lois wished she could do more, but she hadn't been feeling well for several weeks herself. On top of all this, she had two little brothers she had to help take care of. She sighed as she walked. There were so many problems.

Why had God let the grasshoppers come? She couldn't understand; still her faith was strong. Just that morning in family worship her father had said, "As God looked after His people in days gone by, so He will look after us now. Let us keep our trust in Him."

A few weeks before this someone in the family had read in the Bible that God wants His people to pay tithe. He told the rest of the family about it. It meant giving a tenth of their meager income to God. They had talked about it; and they all agreed, that, poor as they were, if God asked for a tenth of their income, they would give it to Him. In the midst of their troubles and poverty, they had begun to pay tithe!

Winter arrived, and the cold weather killed the crawling grasshoppers. But with the return of spring, the question arose, Is it worthwhile planting a garden? Would not the grasshoppers, hatching from the millions of eggs, destroy every sprouting plant before it had a chance to grow?

Grasshoppers or no grasshoppers, Lois's father had the ground prepared. "Surely," he said, "God will do something for us." Yet it seemed foolish to believe. As the plow cut through the earth it turned up thousands of grasshopper eggs just waiting for warm weather to hatch them.

Father had the seeds planted anyway. Soon they sprouted. Little green leaves appeared all over.

But the grasshopper eggs did not hatch. That is, there weren't any grasshoppers in the vegetable patch belonging to Lois's father.

It was uncanny. For there were millions upon millions of grasshoppers everywhere else!

Spring passed into summer. Grasshoppers were so thick in Martin County that it sounded, when they were hopping, like rain falling in a storm. When the grasshoppers rested, they piled up in great heaps.

But still there was not one grasshopper in the vegetable patch where Lois lived. Oh, they tried to get in there. The vegetables on that little patch were the finest in seven counties. But some invisible fence kept them out, some mysterious force chased them back every time they tried to get in.

There was a marvelous crop. From those few acres, Lois's father harvested fifty bushels of beets. Three squash vines alone produced eighty-three large squash!

Word got around. Folks came from far away to buy the choice vegetables, and to marvel at the miracle.

Lois saw it all and wondered. Of course, Father had always said that God would provide. But to keep the grasshoppers away from their patch, when so many other farmers saw all their crops destroyed! To make their vegetables so green and choice and succulent, when on other farms they were brown and stunted and destroyed! It was so very much more than anything she had ever thought God would do!

And why for them? They had never done anything great for God. They weren't missionaries or preachers. They had never risked their lives in God's service.

Then one day someone in the family read Malachi 3:10 and 11: "Bring ye all the tithes into the storehouse, that there may be meat in Mine house, and prove Me now herewith, saith the Lord of hosts, if I will not open you the windows of heaven, and pour you out a blessing, that there shall not be room enough to receive it. And I will rebuke the devourer for your sakes, and he shall not destroy the fruits of your ground."

It seems that the family had never read these verses before. They had learned about tithe paying from Leviticus 27:30–33 or from some of the other tithe texts in the Bible. They had decided to pay tithe simply because God asked for it and not with any idea of getting a reward or blessing.

Now at last Lois understood. They had paid tithe, and God had honored their faith. He had rebuked the devourer and poured them out a blessing.

How humble she felt. God had kept His promise for them, even though no one in the family knew He had made it.

## FIFTY DOLLARS MORE

Mr. Hilton Suddarth is a locomotive engineer. At the time I met him he was driving the big diesels. In older days he operated steam trains.

He told me that in 1929 he ran into serious trouble. Something went wrong at the banks that year. Many people who went to bed one night rich woke up in the morning desperately poor. Millions of workers lost their jobs; and with no wages coming in, their families were soon hungry.

Year after year men walked the streets looking for work. College teachers were happy to dig ditches if only someone would hire them. Highly paid business men were glad to wash windows if some kind soul would give them a few pennies for it.

Mr. Suddarth lost his job, too. And he soon found, as so many others had discovered already, that there weren't any other jobs to be had—not even digging ditches or washing windows.

Then a friend told him there was a chance he could get a job as a bus driver with one of the bus companies in Washington, D.C.

"I know the manager, Mr. May," the friend said. "I'll go with you and introduce you to him, and I'm sure he'll give you the job."

So Mr. Suddarth went with the friend to visit Mr. May, and Mr. May said, "I'll be glad to hire you, Mr. Suddarth. Your pay will be $250.00 a month."

A wonderful wage for those days!

Mr. Suddarth said, "Thank you very much. But before accepting the job I should explain that I am a Seventh-day Adventist and will not be able to work on Saturday."

"I know all about that." Mr. May was so friendly! "You will have to work only the first six Saturdays. After that, everything is already arranged so you can have your Sabbath off every week without fail."

"In that case"—and Mr. Suddarth smiled as warmly as he could—"thank you again, but I'll have to refuse the job."

He got up and walked out. His friend was sure he had now seen every kind of foolishness there was. Imagine a man turning down a job like that just so he could go to church on one particular day of the week—and Saturday, at that!

But Mr. Suddarth remembered that God had promised, "Them that honor Me I will honor." 1 Samuel 2:30. God would do something for him.

And He did—something far better than anything Mr. Suddarth had dared to hope for.

A few nights after he had turned down the bus job, there was a knock on his door. In came a man Mr. Suddarth had never seen.

"I'm a contractor," the stranger explained. "I'm just beginning a large construction job a few miles south of town, and I need someone to look after a million dollars' worth of equipment. I'd like to hire you to be my chief watchman."

"Thank you," Mr. Suddarth said. "But I don't suppose you know that I'm a Seventh-day Adventist. I couldn't work on Saturday."

"On the contrary," the man said, "I know all about your religious beliefs. That's why I want to hire you. You won't need to work on Friday nights or Saturdays, and your salary will be $300.00 a month."

Fifty dollars more than the bus company offered!

Mr. Suddarth took the job. As soon as things eased up, he went back to his locomotives; but he's never for-gotten how God increased his wages when he refused to work on the day the Bible calls "the Sabbath of the Lord thy God."

## WILLIE IN THE WATER

Willie didn't plan to end up in the water. It just worked out that way.

Willie had seen a boat he liked, a plastic one that was so light he could carry it, and just big enough for one person to ride in. At once he began working on Dad to get it for him.

But Dad didn't see eye to eye with his son on this matter. He had heard of too many young fellows who started out in boats and finished up in the water, and when Willie asked him for this boat, Dad said, "No. You're too young for a boat, Willie."

Young or not, Willie had learned that when Dad said No the first time, it paid to keep on asking.

Finally Dad gave in—but there was a catch in the arrangement. Dad said, "You can have one of those boats, Willie, but you'll have to pay for it yourself."

Willie began working on his relatives. He begged from his mother—no success. He begged from his aunts and uncles. No success there, either. He begged from his grandmother. And Grandmother gave him all the money he needed.

Willie got the boat.

Dad was alarmed. There were reasons why he had said No. In his mind, the little boat wasn't safe. In rough water, the passenger could easily fall out. And Willie couldn't swim.

So Dad was extremely relieved when Willie came down with a bad cold the same day the boat arrived.

"Willie," Dad said, "you must not take that boat into the water until your cold is better."

Willie pleaded, but Dad did not change. Not this time. Neither did Mom. She said, "Don't take that boat into the water till your cold is better."

Days passed. Willie was sure his cold was better, but still Mom and Dad said No. Then it began to rain. The little stream behind the house filled up.

What a chance to have fun with my boat, thought Willie.

Dad said, "Under no circumstances, Willie, are you to take your boat out on that creek until this storm is over and the water level has returned to normal."

Then one day Willie came home from school and found the house empty. Mother had been called away to do a special job. And the rain had stopped.

"Now!" shouted Willie.

He grabbed the boat, called to his dog, Hero, and dashed for the creek. Too excited to waste time on ceremony, even for the first launching, he threw the boat onto the waves and climbed aboard.

At once the current swept the tiny craft into the middle of the stream and tipped it over.

Willie was in the water!

"Oh, my boat!" he gasped. He flung out an arm to grab it, and succeeded.

But now what?

He stumbled around and found a large rock. He managed to get up onto it, but when he set out to walk toward the shore, the current tried to sweep him off his feet. So he stood where he was, on that rock, clinging to his precious boat, and shouted, "Help! Help!"

Hero ran up and down the bank and dashed into the water, trying to reach him. But he was only about a year old, scarcely more than a puppy, and he was no match for those angry waters. He turned around and went back.

Willie tried again to walk to the shore, but the minute he stepped off his rock he was in such deep water, he knew he would be swept under. He called for help again and again.

Now, you should know that there are some apartment houses near that creek. Up on the third floor Mrs. Wilkinson heard Willie calling, but she didn't pay any attention. There were hundreds of children in that apartment house, or so it seemed, and a person couldn't run every time one of them called. Besides, Willie didn't need help. He was just playing. And if he did need help, his mother was the one to look after him. She was home. Willie's mother was always home in the afternoon. If she didn't think it important to go and see what was happening, obviously there was nothing serious.

Up on the fourth floor Mr. Perry heard Willie calling, too. But he was quite sure he was calling, "Hero, Hero," and Mr. Perry knew Hero was the name of Willie's dog.

So Mr. Perry went on reading his newspaper, and Mrs. Wilkinson went on dusting her furniture, and poor Willie stood out there on his rock and went on calling for help.

Except that by now he was far more tired than he had been. And cold. He had been standing there nearly half an hour.

The idea came to his mind that perhaps he ought to pray about it. But he had disobeyed his parents. It was his own fault he was in this tough spot. Would God help a boy who had disobeyed?

Willie wasn't sure, but he couldn't stand there much longer. He decided to try God, anyway. He bowed his head.

"Dear God," he prayed, "please help me. I'm sorry I disobeyed Mom and Dad. Please forgive me—and please help me."

He told his mother later, "I prayed three times." And God answered! It seemed to Willie as if someone stood beside him and said, "Call now."

So Willie called. And this time, all sorts of things began to happen!

Mrs. Wilkinson was suddenly alarmed. "That boy's been calling for half an hour! I wonder if his mother's asleep!" She dashed downstairs and began pounding on the door of Willie's apartment.

Mr. Perry suddenly noticed that Willie wasn't calling Hero. "My dear!" he exclaimed to his wife. "I do believe that boy is calling, 'Help!' " He jumped out of his chair, glanced out the window, saw Willie in the water, and leaped for the door. He ran all the way downstairs, and all but bumped into Mrs. Wilkinson, who by this time had decided Willie's mother wasn't home, after all.

Together, the two of them raced for the creek.

Mr. Wilkinson got there first and plunged in. The water came up to his hips and splashed even higher. But he kept right on till he had Willie securely in his arms.

Within minutes after he prayed, Willie was standing on the shore. He was safe. His boat was safe. And Hero was licking him all over.

What a wonderful God we have, to answer our prayers even when we disobey. Surely, in gratitude, we will love Him in return—enough to obey Him always.

# LOST AND FOUND

I listened to two people talking a few days ago. One of them said, "We shouldn't pray about all the little things that happen every day. We should take care of them ourselves, and go to God only for big things."

The other person said, "I believe God is interested in everything we do, and He likes to have us pray about all of them, large or small."

I believe God is interested in the little things as well as the big ones. And here are two stories that prove it. They come from widely separated places in the world, yet they arrived on my desk only four days apart.

Sharon sent me the first one. She lives in Ontario, Canada.

It happened the day she was supposed to take her music lesson. She was feeling a bit nervous in the pit of her stomach, wondering if she could play all her pieces well enough to please her teacher. She gathered up her music and prepared to leave.

Mother said, "Sharon, here is the money to pay your teacher. Put it in your wallet, and be sure you don't lose it."

Now, why do mothers say things like that? Sharon wasn't going to lose that money. Her mother didn't have to tell her to be careful with it.

Her music in her hand and the wallet in a safe place, Sharon said goodbye to Mom and started for the teacher's house.

She had almost reached it, when she discovered she had lost the wallet! She still had all her music, but the wallet, with the teacher's money inside, was gone.

She guessed what the teacher would say.

She had a pretty good idea what her mother would say.

And do!

Oh, dear, she had to find it. She looked all around. She peered under the bushes. She even poked around in the leaves to see if somehow the wallet had slipped under them.

But there was no wallet.

In her letter she said, "Suddenly I thought about praying. I knelt down right there and prayed that Jesus would help me find my wallet."

When you think of all the great, important things God has to look after, all the suns in the universe that He must keep burning, and all the worlds that circle around them that He must take care of, a girl's lost wallet is a very little thing.

Would the great God, sitting on His throne and ruling the vast universe, help a girl find her wallet?

Sharon finished her prayer and opened her eyes, and she told me, "I saw my wallet by a bush."

God had helped her!

She was so glad she knelt down right there and thanked Him.

There is no doubt in Sharon's mind that God is interested in even the little things of our lives. There shouldn't be any doubt in your mind, either.

The second story came from Andrew.

Andrew wanted a camera. And his parents were willing—providing he bought it with his own 'money.

So Andrew saved, and by the beginning of the summer he had enough. He bought the camera, and with it he purchased four rolls of film, two of them for colored pictures.

Andrew lives in England. The family decided that for their summer vacation they would take a trip through Dorset County, on the southwest coast.

They hitched their caravan onto the back of their car, to sleep in at night. (A caravan is what the English call a trailer.) And Andrew took his camera.

One day they came to Corfe Castle, a grand old ruin, where a fellow can imagine all sorts of exciting things.

Andrew and his sister, Stella, climbed all over it. Andrew took several pictures. Then Dad said, "Back to the car! We have many more places to see."

Andrew and Stella got into the car. And that's when Andrew made the agonizing discovery.

His camera was gone!

All plans for further traveling were immediately abandoned. Everybody got out of the car and began to search. They climbed all over the castle again. But they didn't find the camera.

They went to the police station and reported the loss. And that night, Andrew said in the letter he sent me, "I returned to our caravan to sleep, a disappointed boy."

Then the thought came to him, "Pray about it." But does God help boys find lost cameras?

It wasn't a very expensive camera. To be sure, Andrew had had to save quite a long time to buy it. But when you think how much some cameras cost, this wasn't a very fancy one at all. Would God use the tremendous, miraculous powers of heaven to help locate a cheap camera like that?

Well, let's see what He did for Andrew.

Andrew wrote me, "That night I prayed to Jesus about my camera, asking Him to look after it for me and to keep it safe. Morning and evening I prayed, and sometimes during the day. I prayed that Jesus would put it in the heart of the finder to hand it in at the police station."

Three days went by.

Then a message was delivered to the caravan site: "Would Andrew please call at the police station."

Andrew's letter says, "We had gone out when this call came through, so we did not hear of it till the evening. While Mother and my sister, Stella, prepared the evening meal, Daddy took me to the police station seven miles away. We found my camera waiting for me. A young girl had found it and decided to keep it, but after having it in her possession three days she decided to try to find the owner."

What a remarkable experience! There is a story in the Bible about a time when Daniel prayed that the Israelites might be delivered from bondage. God sent an angel to talk to the king of Persia and persuade him to change his mind and let the Israelites go. You expect God to do something like that when Daniel prayed. Daniel was such a famous man.

But the amazing thing is that God did exactly the same thing when Andrew prayed—He sent an angel to talk to that girl who found his camera, and to persuade her to give it back. Yet Andrew was only eight years old!

In the last story I told you about Willie, and how God saved him from drowning in the creek. That was in America. Then I told you how God helped Sharon find her wallet. That was in Canada. Now I've told you how God helped Andrew—in England.

Surely, as the Bible says, "The eyes of the Lord run to and fro throughout the whole earth, to show Himself strong in the behalf of them" who love Him. 2 Chronicles 16:9.

You can always take all your problems to Him.

## BOB'S MISSING SHOES

Bob attended a private boarding school. He had just been to the shoe store and bought a brand-new pair of black shoes. He sat on the edge of his bed in the school dormitory and gazed down at them.

"What beauties!" he whispered. "I won't wear them today. I think I'll wear them first for church tomorrow. They'll go well with my best suit."

He bent over and picked up one of them and held it in front of him. The shine on the toe was so bright he could almost see his face in it. Then he turned the shoe over and stroked the sole with his finger. It had never been walked on and was smooth and shiny, too.

"Well, better not sit here all day," he muttered at last. "I'll put them in the closet so no one will step on them."

He picked them up lovingly and placed them in the back of the closet; then he changed into his work clothes.

Morning dawned. Bob opened his eyes. He frowned, trying to think. "There was something nice going to happen to me today," he whispered. "What was it?

What was—Ah! My shoes. I wear my new shoes today. I hope it isn't raining."

A glance out the window revealed a perfectly clear sky. He jumped out of bed and ran to the closet. He reached down for the shoes.

They weren't there!

"Hey, Sam!" he called to his roommate. "What happened to my shoes?"

"Your shoes?" Sam mumbled with his face in his pillow. "I don't know anything about your shoes."

"Well!" Bob said. "They've disappeared, and they couldn't possibly have walked away by themselves."

He went back and looked under his bed. They weren't there. He returned to the closet and moved things around. Still no shoes.

"Sam, did you see anyone in the room messing with my stuff?" He felt like crying.

Sam yawned. "No, can't say I did."

"Come on, Sam! Get with it, can't you?" Bob was growing more and more upset. "Those shoes cost me money, and I can't afford another pair. Can't you help me find them?"

Sam sat on the edge of his bed and stretched, then he yawned again.

"Oh, phooey on you!" Bob exclaimed, and he dashed out of the room to see if some of his other friends would be more helpful.

The shoes were not found. Bob had to go to church in his old ones. Weeks went by. Still no shoes. Then one day, when Bob went to his closet to get something, there were the shoes sitting where he had left them.

"Hey, Sam!" he called to his roommate. "What do you know! My shoes are back!"

Sam smiled. "Sure, I knew that. I had them all the time."

"You—had—them—all—the—time!" Bob said the words slowly, so that each one came out separate from the others. "Are you a thief or something?"

Sam bristled. "Don't you dare call me that!" His face was suddenly red with anger. "I didn't steal your shoes. It was just a prank—a schoolboy joke."

"Maybe that's what you call it." Bob looked Sam in the eye. "But taking something as expensive as my new shoes and keeping it for as long as you kept my shoes, even though you knew how much I needed them, is a very unfunny kind of joke. Do you want me to tell the principal about it, so he can laugh too?"

Sam hissed, "Don't you dare!"

"But if it's only a joke, why not? Or would you have kept the shoes if they'd been your size? Answer me that one if you can."

Sam went out and slammed the door behind him.

Bob thought to himself, I really ought to tell the principal. If Sam did not plan to steal the shoes, why was he so touchy? Some of the other fellows in the dormitory have been complaining that their things are missing. Has Sam played some of his "jokes" on them too? But Bob hated to tell tales on his roommate.

Winter turned into spring. Things continued to disappear from the dormitory. A few turned up again, others did not. Some of the boys suspected Sam, but he was never punished.

Bob finished school and graduated, and the years went by. He heard no more of Sam, till one day he went back to that school for a class reunion. One of his old buddies said, "I think you ought to visit Sam."

"Sure," Bob said. "I'd love to. Where's he living?" "If you can call it living, he's living at the county jail. He was booked for stealing."

Bob went to visit his old roommate, glad they weren't roommates now.

As he left the jail, he thought, perhaps Sam really did mean it as a joke when he took my shoes. I never could convince him it wasn't very funny. Now look at him. Strange, the way habits we think are harmless while we are young can get us into trouble when we grow up. Poor Sam!

## COONS IN THE CORN

The moon was shining bright out of a clear sky, and the corn was ripe.

The raccoons' little noses twitched with excitement. It was a night for a feast. Forth went the furry army, and down came the corn. Next morning, the farmers looked out with dismay on the havoc they had wrought.

Among these farmers was one just eleven years old. Jerry lives in Colorado. At his church, all the members of the junior division were given an opportunity to borrow up to five dollars to invest for missions.

"I will lend you one or two dollars—up to five," the leader said, "and you may buy something with it. You might buy seeds and plant them, or you might buy cloth and make something useful from it. Then sell your fruit or the things you have made. Return the money you borrowed, and give your profit to the mission offering."

Jerry borrowed the full five dollars and spent it planting half an acre to sweet corn.

Now the coons had gotten into his corn. He went to see his father about it. "How come the coons ate my corn?" he asked. "You told me I ought to pay tithe, and I promised I would. So why didn't God rebuke the devourer as He said He would? They ate twenty ears; I counted them."

"Son," Father said, "you have planted your seed, and you have promised to pay tithe on what you earn. All right then, don't worry. God will bless your crop in a special way, and He will rebuke the devourer, just as He promised in Malachi, chapter 3. You wait and see. He'll keep his word."

It sounded strange for Dad to say God would rebuke the devourer, when God had already let the coons get twenty ears. But Jerry decided to be patient.

The summer wore on. The coons came back several times to Jerry's half acre.

The summer wore on. The coons ate corn, lots of it. Many farmers lost more than half of their crop. The coons came back several times to Jerry's half acre.

The corn ripened. Jerry picked some of it. One of Jerry's friends told me what had happened. She said, "Jerry got seventy-five dozen ears from just one picking. He sold some to a store at 35 cents a dozen, and the rest in the neighborhood for 40 cents a dozen."

From that one picking Jerry received more than $25.

And the corn kept getting ripe. Jerry filled a can with money from his sales; then he filled another, and still the coins spilled over, and he had to use a quart jar.

Finally all the corn was sold. Jerry counted his money and returned the five dollars and paid tithe on his profit. Then he turned in the rest for the mission offering—$114.36. All that, from five dollars!

But why did God allow the coons to get into Jerry's corn? Let's see about this. Many farmers lost more than half their crops that summer.

The coons took twenty ears from Jerry's half acre the first night. During the summer they ate about two dozen more—not quite four dozen altogether.

God doesn't like to see the wild animals go hungry. He loves them, too. So he gave the raccoons forty-four, ears of Jerry's corn. Then he gave Jerry 350 dozen ears that He didn't let the coons touch. That's forty-four ears for the raccoons and 4,200 ears for Jerry.

Jerry was so excited about the whole experience that he planned to get more seed to sow next spring as soon as the weather would be warm enough.

## PIECE, PACE, AND PEACE

It was time for the spelling test. "Remember," said the teacher, "today we are going to see if there is any row in which all the students get 100 percent."

Patricia wrote the words carefully as the teacher read them off. She was sure she got them all right, except for "piece." Or was it "peice"? Was the rule, "I before e," or, "E before i"? Oh, dear!

She wrote the word one way, and it didn't look right; she erased it and wrote it the other way. Still it didn't look right.

The test over, the teacher told the class to exchange papers. Patricia handed hers to the girl in front and hoped for the best.

A few minutes later, the girl in front handed the paper back. "Oh, goody," Patricia sighed. There, in large figures, she saw "100%."

"But did I really spell 'piece' right?" she wondered. What was this? Checking the word carefully, she was sure someone had written "ie" where she had apparently put "ei." "It must have been the girl in front," she concluded. "She wanted everyone in our row to have a perfect score, so she corrected my spelling."

Patricia glanced over the rest of the words and found another one spelled wrong, which the girl in front had overlooked. She didn't have 100 percent. She had two wrong.

Should she tell the teacher? If she did, it would look as though the girl in front had cheated. And then, too, her row wouldn't get a perfect score.

If only she had more time to think. But already the teacher was calling for the scores. "Anne? Henry? Jack?

Jane?" he went down the list. Before she had decided what to do, he called, "Patricia?"

Patricia said, "One hundred."

And at once she knew she had lied.

It bothered her all day. "You're a cheat, Patricia," a voice seemed to say. "Just a sneaking cheat. You said you had a hundred when you had two wrong. You're a cheat, Patricia, just a sneaking—"

When she went to bed that night, the memory of what she had done still haunted her. Voices all around the room seemed to be chanting, "You said you had a hundred when you had two wrong. You're a cheat, Patricia. You said you had a hundred—"

Long after Mother thought her daughter was asleep she was surprised to hear a voice calling, "Mother, please come here."

There was despair in the voice, and Mother ran upstairs. Sitting on Patricia's bed she asked, "What's the matter, dear?"

Slowly, painfully, Patricia told her everything.

"But what shall I do now?" she said when she had finished. "If I tell the teacher, he'll never trust me again."

"You must tell him," Mother said gently. "But I'm sure he'll respect you for it."

It took a lot of courage, but Patricia told the teacher next morning. He said he was proud of her for owning up. And so was I when I heard of it, and that's why I am telling this story to you.

If there is something you ought to make right, hurry and confess it. Don't let little things like *peice* shatter your *peace* all to *pieces*!

## THE SHOEMAKER'S HAMMER

The shoemaker adjusted the shoe carefully and slipped a nail from between his teeth. He set it exactly where he wanted it to go in the shoe and struck it with his hammer. But as the hammer came down on the nail, the hammer's iron head broke in two.

"It is the sign of the Lord!" the shoemaker cried.

This shoemaker lived in Spain. Let's call him Señor Menon, for I do not know his real name; though the story certainly happened, and not very long ago.

Señor Menon was a poor shoemaker, so poor, indeed, that he owned only two hammers. He also had a radio, which kept him company while he worked.

One day, over this radio, came the sound of a quartet singing, "Lift up the trumpet, and loud let it ring." Then a man talked about the love of God and some of the other important things that the Bible teaches.

"Good sermon, good singing," Señor Menon muttered to himself. "I must tune in again next week."

He heard the program many times. The more he heard it, the more he liked it. Then into his shop one morning came a man selling books.

Señor Menon examined the salesman's wares. "How interesting!" he exclaimed. "These books say the same things I hear on the radio every week."

"You mean, on the Voice of Prophecy program?" the salesman asked.

"The very one," the shoemaker replied. "I listen every week. In fact, I know by now just about everything those Voice of Prophecy people teach. I have a few questions, though."

"Well, now," the book salesman said, "it just happens that I'm quite well acquainted with the Voice of Prophecy myself, and if you wish, I'll be glad to have a friend of mine who works at the Voice of Prophecy office come around to your house and visit you."

The shoemaker liked the idea. So every evening for several days the salesman's friend visited the shoemaker, and the two men studied the Bible together, along with Señor Menon's wife.

Señor Menon felt he could agree with everything—except just one point.

"This Sabbath business—" He shook his head. "You say that Saturday is the Sabbath, and not Sunday. All my life I've been told it was the other way around. And I've worked on Saturday since I was a boy. You can't tell me God says we shouldn't work on Saturday."

The salesman's friend reached for Señor Menon's Bible and turned the pages till he, had found a certain text. He handed the Book back to the shoemaker.

"We read this verse just a few minutes ago." He spoke slowly and quietly. "Read it again, in your own Bible: 'The seventh day is the sabbath of the Lord thy God: thou shalt do no work on it.' [Exodus 20:10, Douay.] Isn't that clear?"

"Yes, yes, it is clear." Señor Menon was thoughtful. "It is very clear. And it is God who said it. Wife," he squeezed her hand, "we must begin to keep the Lord's Sabbath."

There were tears in Señora Menon's eyes. "I've felt that way for several days, dear."

"Then that's the way it will be." Señor Menon held out a hand to the salesman's friend. "Thank you for bringing us God's truth and telling us what He says in His Word."

For a moment it seemed as if the salesman's friend didn't know what to say, but then he asked Señor and Señora Menon to kneel, and he prayed for them that God would keep them faithful.

Saturday morning arrived, the first Saturday Señor Menon was to keep as the Sabbath.

Great waves of doubt swept over him. What had he done? Why had he promised that salesman's friend he would keep Saturday holy? Why had he said he would not work but go to church instead? All his life he had worked on Saturday, and his father had, and so had his grandfather and his great-grandfather, as far back as he knew.

Besides, there was a huge pile of shoes at the shop that needed to be repaired. He had promised his customers they would be ready on Monday, yet here it was Saturday, and he hadn't finished them yet. His customers would come expecting to find them finished and would be angry when they had to go away without them. Probably they would take their worn shoes to some other shoemaker next time.

"Wife," he said, "I won't be going with you to church this morning. I have to work."

The sparkle faded from her eyes.

"I'm sorry, dear," he said. "It won't happen again. It's just that there are so many shoes I haven't finished yet, and the customers will be calling for them on Monday. We made our decision to keep this Saturday holy too near the end of the week. I didn't have enough time to get the work done. But by next Saturday it will be different. I will have all week to plan, so I'll have everything done by Friday night."

He grabbed his cap and hurried out of the house so he could get away from that expression in his wife's eyes.

Arriving at the shop, Señor Menon sat down on his stool. He picked up a shoe and adjusted it on a last. He picked up one of his two hammers and drove in several nails. He had begun every working day this way for so many years he didn't even think about it anymore.

To finish the shoe he had to use the second hammer. He reached for it.

He didn't look. He didn't need to. The hammer was always in the same place. He could have found it in the dark.

But this morning, when his hand closed to grip that second hammer, there wasn't any hammer there! Señor Menon glanced up, startled.

The place where that hammer always lay was empty! He looked along the whole length of the bench. No hammer.

He swung down off his stool and gazed around his little workshop. He searched high and low. The second hammer was nowhere to be found.

Well! He had to finish the shoes. He struggled with them all day, but without the second hammer it was hard.

And all the time something seemed to be saying, "God is trying to speak to you. He hid your hammer for a sign that Saturday is His holy day, and you should worship him on it."

"But a lost hammer couldn't be a sign from God," he argued. "I lose things all the time. Am I supposed to change my religion every time I can't find something?"

The wonder of it was, however, that on Monday morning the second hammer was on the bench, right where it was supposed to be.

"That shows it wasn't really lost," Señor Menon decided. "It was there all the time; I just couldn't see it.

Every day that week Señor Menon worked as usual, and always when he reached for the second hammer it was where he expected it to be.

As hard as he worked, by Friday night there was a great stack of shoes not yet finished. He would have to work on Saturday again.

His wife pleaded with him. She reminded him of his promise the week before. He assured her it wouldn't happen anymore.

That Sabbath morning, the second hammer was missing!

Señor Menon felt a chill sweep through him. "This is strange indeed! Is it a sign from the Lord?" He shivered. "No, it couldn't be! What's so important about losing a hammer?"

He sat down on his stool. He still had one hammer. He kept an eye on it as he made himself comfortable. He didn't want to lose it, too!

He adjusted a shoe carefully on one of the lasts.

A quick glance at the hammer. He popped a handful of nails into his mouth, arranged them with his tongue, and then with two fingers of his left hand slipped a nail from between his teeth and put it exactly where he wanted it in the shoe.

He looked again at the hammer. It was still in its proper place.

He picked it up. It felt solid in his hand. Nothing was going to happen to this one!

He raised the hammer above the nail. He brought the hammer down against the nail—and the iron head broke in two.

That's when Señor Menon exclaimed, "It is the sign of the Lord! One of my hammers refused to work last Sabbath, and now my other hammer has refused to work today. If they won't work on Saturday, neither will I."

He left everything as it was, closed his little shop, and hurried home to tell his wife.

As soon as possible after that, the two of them were baptized into membership in the church that sponsors the Voice of Prophecy program.

When the ceremony was over, the minister handed Señor Menon a gift.

"Here's a new hammer," he said. "I am sure it will never work on God's Sabbath."

Señor Menon smiled. "I assure you, it most certainly will not."

And it never has.

## NANCY'S MATH PROBLEM

Nancy knew she couldn't do the math assignment, the minute the teacher told the class what their homework would be.

Not only was it a long assignment, but it was full of word problems. And No. 8 was a real sticker. She could tell by how many lines it stretched down the page.

The teacher was writing the assignment on the board. He turned and faced the class. "Oh, yes, class." The smile grew broader. "That No. 8 will probably challenge all of you."

That was the way Mr. Hiller was. He never said a problem was hard. He would call it "challenging" or "interesting," or something like that. And he always seemed to get the greatest pleasure out of watching the class sweat over one of them.

Nancy knew how she would describe such problems. "Impossible." She certainly couldn't see anything to smile about.

She didn't realize how worried she looked till Georgine, her best friend, stopped by her desk to walk home with her.

"Cheer up!" Georgine exclaimed. "You look like the victim of some great calamity."

"Oh, Georgine, I am." Nancy gathered her books while she talked. "I can't possibly do that math assignment, especially that awful No. 8. Why does he have to give us problems like that? You know I'm the class dunce."

"Is that what's bothering you!" Georgine tossed her head. "Don't worry about it. I don't suppose any of us will get all the assignment perfect."

Nancy spoke hardly a word on the way home. She got down to her homework as soon as she could. She did her English and geography first. She always liked them, especially English. There was a composition to write tonight, and she loved writing compositions best of all.

But then there was the math assignment. It loomed like a great, impenetrable wall of darkness, like a jungle full of snakes and sharp-toothed beasts and creeping things.

She shuddered as she opened the textbook. But the job had to be done, and she went at it. It wasn't as bad as she had feared! In an hour or so she had the first seven problems. She looked at the eighth and decided to skip it for a while. She went on and did nine and ten.

Nearly done! She read through No. 8. Number 8 was simply unworkable!

Still, she stuck with it. She didn't realize how the hours were passing till she felt Mother standing beside her.

"It's long past bedtime, dear."

"But, Mother, I can't go to bed yet. I still have this problem to do." In spite of herself, her voice broke. Mother smiled down at her. "Have you prayed about it, Nancy?"

"But, Mom, would that do any good?"

"I think so, dear. I am sure God would like to help you. You know, He says in the Bible, 'If any of you lack wisdom, let him ask of God, that giveth to all men liberally;...and it shall be given him.' That's in the first chapter of James. I'm sure God will help you if you ask Him. Run along upstairs to bed, and when you pray, ask God about this problem."

Nancy went upstairs slowly. She put on her pajamas and knelt by her bed, as she always did before getting in. She said her prayers in the usual way. Then she paused. "Dear Lord," she whispered, "please help me with No. 8. I've done the best I know how, and I can't get it, and Mother says You'll help me. Please, if You don't mind, please do. Amen."

She jumped into bed and was asleep in no time.

Almost immediately, it seemed, she was awake again. It was morning. And right there in her mind, clear as daylight, was the answer to that math problem.

"Oh, thank You, Jesus!" She almost sang the words. She ran downstairs and wrote it all out. It was the right answer, complete and perfect. "Thank You, dear Lord. Thank You so very, very much."

She hummed while she cleaned her teeth, she sang while she washed her face, she kept breaking into little chuckles of laughter as she ate her breakfast, and she talked a blue streak to Georgine all the way to school.

Many years later Nancy said to some friends, "That was the first time I discovered that God would help me solve my problems if I would pray."

When Nancy reached school that morning she could hardly wait for math class to begin. Every once in a while she caught herself smiling. She kept saying to herself, I know the answer to No. 8 and I'm sure nobody else does.

Unless maybe Allen does.

Allen was the class whiz. He never missed a math problem.

Well, then, she thought, possibly Allen has it. But no one else. I'm almost positive. And besides, Allen is a boy.

Math class—at last! Mr. Hiller stood beside his desk. "Does anyone have any questions on last night's assignment?" He gazed over the room. "How about No. 8?" He smiled that same, coy little smile he wore yesterday, only today it was broader. "Did anyone solve No. 8?"

Nancy felt her face burn. She glanced around. Not one single hand was up! Allen sat in the row behind her on the other side of the room. She turned around enough to look at him. His hand was down!

So Allen didn't have the answer. Not even Allen! Mr. Hiller repeated his question. "Did anyone solve No. 8? No one at all?"

Then Georgine began to talk. Some friend, she was! "Mr. Hiller, I think Nancy has the answer. She tole me so on the way to school this morning."

Nancy could have laughed out loud at what happened to Mr. Hiller's face right then. His eyes seemed to pop out, and his jaw fell.

But then he recovered, blinked a couple of times, and smiled again.

"Uh, Nancy, do you really think you have the answer?"

Nancy shot an ungrateful glance at Georgine and said, "Yes, Mr. Hiller."

"Well, now, that's— uh, that's excellent, Nancy. Would you please come up and do the problem on the board so we can all see how it's done?"

Oh, no! Not on the board! All of a sudden Nancy's confidence vanished. Perhaps her answer wasn't right. Perhaps she had been too sure.

And then she reasoned, I asked God to help me. I couldn't have gotten the answer by myself, so He must have helped me, and He certainly wouldn't give me a wrong answer.

She noticed that the class had grown quiet, and everyone was watching her.

She walked to the front as bravely as she could. She began to write. Every part of the problem fitted together. As she wrote the final number, she knew the answer was absolutely perfect.

Georgine called out, "Good for you, Nancy!" Allen gasped, "Wow!"

Nancy glowed!

As for Mr. Hiller, he looked surprised—and tremendously impressed.

"That was excellent, Nancy," he exclaimed. "Excellent! I didn't know you had it in you."

Oh! but Nancy was walking on air when she went home that night! She started her homework with math this time. She could do math, and she knew she could. She could even get answers the others couldn't.

However, the assignment tonight was rather hard. There were no problems as difficult as that No. 8 had been, but she decided she'd better leave math and get on with English and science and geography.

She finished them quickly and went back to math. "I'll work on math as hard as I can till bedtime, then I'll pray, and in the morning I'll have the answer."

There were a couple of problems still unsolved at bedtime. Nancy prayed about them. In the morning she had the right answers.

It went on like this for several days. Nancy's grades in math began to climb spectacularly. Oh, but math was a delightful subject!

It was so easy

And it was her praying that was making the difference. But Nancy still had something else to learn about prayer.

A week or ten days after Nancy solved problem No. 8, she got a new storybook at school. After school she crept up to her bedroom quietly so Mother wouldn't know she was home, and read till supper.

After supper Mother said, "You'd better get at your homework, dear."

"Yes, Mother," Nancy replied—and went on reading.

She glanced at the clock. It was getting late. Just one more chapter. After all, she told herself, I don't have to study as hard as I used to. I know how to get answers to my problems now. I have a little servant inside me, and when I pray he works all night and tells me the answers in the morning.

Long past her usual bedtime, Nancy closed the book and turned to her assignments. Math didn't look particularly difficult. Certainly none of the problems were any harder than some she had been solving recently. "I'll pray about them," she decided. "Then I'll write the answers when I wake up."

So she prayed and went to sleep.

Mother was standing in the bedroom door.

"Wake up, Nancy. I've called you twice already. It's way past time to get dressed."

Nancy struggled out of bed. She saw her books where she had left them.

Oh, dear, there were all those math problems she hadn't done! And her brain was full of cobwebs! Other mornings, after she had prayed the night before, she could always think clearly. But not today.

She sat at her table and yawned. She looked at the first problem. It was so hard! She ought to be eating breakfast right now, and she wasn't even dressed. "Please, Lord," she pleaded. "Tell me what the answers are."

Little mice of panic ran around inside her stomach. "Dear God, I prayed last night. You've got to help me! Please!"

Still there was no answer.

"Nancy! I want to hear the water running in the bathroom!"

Mother again!

Nancy pulled on her clothes. She trudged to school. If only teacher would forget math class today!

She managed to work a few problems at odd times between classes, but most of her answers were wrong. The grade she got was terrible, simply terrible.

"And that was the experience," Nancy told her friends later, "that taught me another vital thing about prayer. God doesn't promise to answer prayers for lazy people. We must stretch ourselves to the limit. Since then I've combined work and prayer, and God has helped me in many wonderful ways."

# THREE SIPS OF BEER

Margie's mother died when Margie was twelve years old.

Margie had an older sister, and there was still Dad, of course. But without Mother the home broke up. Margie was sent to live with one of her aunts.

Auntie and Uncle treated her well. Almost too well, in fact. They loved to drink beer. And being kind-hearted, they wanted Margie to drink with them.

"Come, Margie," Auntie would say. "Here's a glass of beer for you. You'll like it; it tastes so good."

It was hard to refuse such a kind, generous aunt. But Margie kept remembering something her mother had said to her.

Just before she died, Mother had called her to her bedside and said, "Margie, please promise me you will always do what you know is right, and be a good, faithful Christian all your life. Promise me, too, that you will never, never drink anything with alcohol in it."

Margie had promised. Her mother had talked to her about beer and wine and whiskey many times. She had read to her from the Bible, "Wine is a mocker, strong drink is raging: and whosoever is deceived thereby is not wise." Proverbs 20:1.

Mother had told her, too, how beer and wine often make people do foolish things, and how very often people who begin drinking end up with their money gone and their health ruined.

Every time the aunt offered her a glass of beer, Margie always refused.

When her father heard what was happening, he took Margie away from those relatives and put her in the home of some others. Soon after that she was moved to yet another place, and then to another. So it went.

In one of the homes where Margie stayed, the man and his wife liked to invite friends over for the evening and would give them light refreshments, including beer. Margie had to serve these refreshments.

One evening, after she had served the guests, she walked back into the kitchen with the dirty dishes and noticed in the bottom of the beer pail about a tablespoonful of beer.

She thought, Why do people like beer so much? It smells horrible. Does it taste better than it smells? I wish I knew.

What would happen if I tasted the beer in the bottom of this pail? I promised Mother I'd never drink anything like this. But maybe just a sip would be all right. Yes, I think Mother wouldn't really mind.

She dipped a spoon into the beer in the bottom of that beer pail and poured a little of it into her mouth — just a teeny little sip.

She wrinkled her face. "What a flavor! Ugh!" She spat it out at once and drank some water quickly to wash the taste away.

"Well," she gasped, "I won't ever do that again!"

She didn't realize that when a person does something wrong, no matter how much he regrets it afterward, it is always easier to do wrong a second time.

A few evenings later Margie had to serve refreshments again. Once more the guests did not quite finish all the beer, and there was a little left in the bottom of the pail, the same as before.

Once more the thought came to her, "What does beer taste like? Surely what I sipped the first time must have gone bad. Beer can't really be like that, or no one would drink it."

She took a sip—her second one. It was easier this time. She spat it out! "What a terrible taste! I'm never going to try beer again."

But those two sips had done something to her mind, though she didn't realize it yet.

A few nights later there was another party. Once more Margie served the guests, and once more there was a little beer left in the pail.

Margie quite forgot that she had decided never to taste beer again.

She quite forgot what she had promised her mother. She didn't stop to argue with herself at all. She went ahead and tasted the beer—her third sip.

And it tasted wonderful! "Now I can see why people are so crazy about beer! It really does taste good!"

Suddenly she realized what had been happening.

"Oh, dear." She sobbed. "I used to hate beer; now I've learned to like it. Dear Jesus," she prayed, "I'm sorry for what I've done. Please forgive me—and help me never to take another sip as long as I live. Help me keep my promise to my mother."

This happened many years ago. Margie is grown-up now. In fact, she is a grandmother, and some of her grandchildren are married.

I was talking to her one night. "Did you ever drink again?" I asked her.

"No!" she snapped. "I most certainly did not. I never drank another sip of beer in my life."

She went on. "Tell the juniors and teenagers you meet that the great enemy of souls is out to get them. He was trying to trap me back then when I was fourteen years old. He nearly caught me, too. I'm so glad I had already given my heart to God, and He wouldn't let me go."

## BAD TASTE IN HIS MOUTH

Dick was courting Jane, and things were going well. He could almost hear the wedding bells ringing already.

But he had reckoned without Jane's dad.

For Dick smoked, and Jane's dad called tobacco "filthy stuff." "No daughter of mine," he said, "will ever marry a man who smokes."

One night when Dick was visiting Jane, Dad decided to act.

"Dick," he said, "I wish you'd stop smoking. It's a dirty, filthy habit."

Dick wasn't surprised. He already knew how Dad felt. He answered respectfully, "I'm sorry it bothers you, sir. I enjoy smoking."

Dad said, "How can you enjoy it? Haven't you been reading the newspapers? Don't you know that smoking causes lung cancer? that thousands upon thousands of people die every year because of it?"

"Sure, I've read all that," Dick said. "But hardly anyone my age ever gets cancer. I'll stop before I'm old enough."

Dad scowled. "It may not be as easy to stop as you think, young man. You should break the habit now. Every pack of cigarettes shortens a smoker's life. If you keep on smoking at the rate you're going, you'll probably die ten years sooner than you would otherwise, even if you don't get lung cancer."

Dick smiled. "I'll worry about that later, if you don't mind. What difference will it make if I only live to be seventy instead of eighty?"

Dad looked quite distressed. Very solemnly he said, "Has no one told you that it is written in the Bible that you shouldn't smoke?"

"Oh, come now," Dick said. "You don't 'really mean that, do you?"

"I most certainly do," Dad said. "I'll make a bargain with you. If I can show you that the Bible says you shouldn't smoke, will you promise to quit?"

"Well, I guess so," Dick agreed. "I wouldn't want to go against anything that's in the Bible. But I don't think you can show me any such thing."

Dad got a Bible and looked for his text. "Here it is, 1 Corinthians 3:17: 'If any man defile the temple of God, him shall God destroy; for the temple of God is holy, which temple ye are.' There, that proves it."

"But, er, why do you say that text means you shouldn't smoke?" Dick said.

"Of course it does," Dad said. "God says we must not do anything that defiles our bodies. Breathing smoke into the body—that's a filthy habit, no doubt about it. And don't forget all those tobacco tars the TV advertisements keep talking about. Look at your fingers, will you? They've already been stained by nicotine. Your breath smells, and so do your clothes, all the time. I don't know how Jane can stand to be near you. Yes, most certainly smoking defiles the body. So that proves it. The Bible says we mustn't smoke. Let us pray."

"Come now," Dick objected. "Let's not pray. I don't want to quit."

"Let's pray anyway," Dad said. "You kneel down there, and I'll kneel here."

Dick couldn't get out of it, so he knelt.

Dad prayed. He asked God to help Dick realize the terrible things smoking was doing to him and to help him break the habit and leave tobacco alone.

They stood up. Dick was grinning; but he felt it wouldn't be polite to say out loud what he was thinking about poor old Dad.

After a while he said "Good night" to Jane and went out to his car. First thing, he lit up a cigarette. But something was wrong.

"What an awful taste!" He spat out the cigarette. He tried another, but it tasted as bad as the first. He opened another pack and tried one from it. It tasted the same. Simply dreadful!

"Whatever has happened?" he wondered.

Then he remembered Dad's prayer—and stared into space, thinking. Did Dad's prayer have anything to do with this bad taste?

All this happened years ago. Today Dick is sure it was God's way of answering Dad's prayer that made those cigarettes taste so bad. From that day to this, even the smell of tobacco smoke has given him a bad taste in his mouth, and he has never smoked again.

Dick tells everyone he knows that God considers smoking a filthy habit.

And, oh, yes; he did marry Jane!

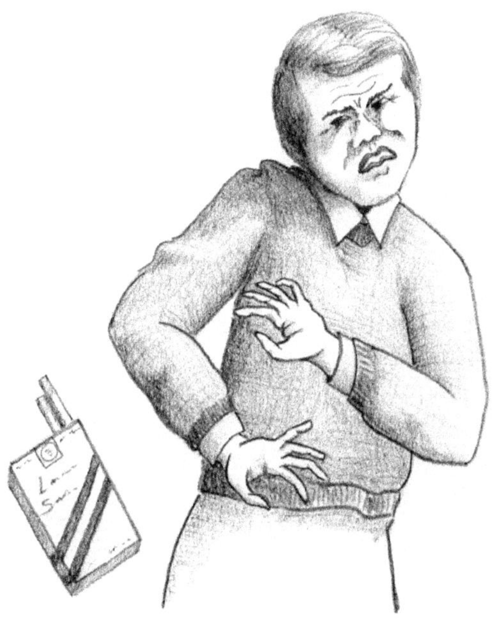

# MY CAR HAD BAD HABITS

Some years ago I bought myself a brand-new car, It was light blue on the lower parts and dark blue on the roof.

It was a good car all the time it was young. But after I had had it a few years, I noticed a change. The car began to have trouble with several bad habits. It took up smoking. Smoke would pour out the back, and when I would stop at a red light, smoke would billow up from under the hood.

About the same time I noticed that the old car had begun to drink. I was asked to visit a summer camp to speak to the campers. The camp was only about two hundred miles away, and a new car could have made the trip on less than one tankful. But on that particular trip I had to fill the tank three times.

Along about the same time, I noticed that the car was having trouble with its dress. Many rusty spots showed through the paint.

And argue! How that car would argue! Sometimes I'd have to work the starter button ten minutes or more before the engine would start.

It became very reluctant to go to church. On one occasion I was asked to preach at a distant church. I started to drive to the town. When I was about five miles from the church the car stopped, and nothing under the sun would get it to move again. I had to take the carburetor apart and put it back together before the car would go. Even then, the engine stopped again before I quite reached the church, and I had to walk the last of the way.

Well, what do you do with an old car like that? I didn't want to get rid of it, so I tried to fix it. I started with dress. I took my car to church—I mean, to the garage—and had it repainted from front to back and top to bottom. It looked great—just like a new car. But it wasn't a new car. It still smoked and it still drank and it still argued.

I decided to work on the smoking and drinking. I asked a friend of mine to take the engine apart and grind the valves and install new piston rings. He did, and the smoking and drinking stopped. For a while. But it was still an old car. And it still argued.

I decided after a few months that the car argued because there was something wrong with the carburetor. I bought new parts for the carburetor and put them in, but that did no good. I bought two rebuilt carburetors one after the other, but neither of them helped.

And by this time the engine had backslid. It was smoking again, worse than before. And drinking again, too. I hired a professional and had him go to work. He did a good job, and the smoking stopped.

But it was right about then that the transmission gave out. I was driving home over some hills. It was just about midnight, and I was on a lonely road with the car full of passengers, when the engine suddenly began to race and the car stopped.

Well, I got the transmission fixed—and I put on new tires and new seat covers. But still it was an old car. And now the steering was going bad.

So after I'd spent about five hundred dollars on repairs in six months, I finally sold the car for $250 to a mechanic who knew its problems—and I bought a new car.

What a change! The new car didn't have any dress problems. It didn't have any smoking or drinking problems. It didn't argue. It went everywhere I wanted it to go, and it went willingly. Blessings be on that new car. It didn't argue!

It helped me to see what Jesus meant when He said, "Ye must be born again."

Paint and seat covers and new tires and rebuilt carburetors won't make an old car into a new one. No more than tying oranges onto an apple tree will make an apple tree into an orange tree.

No more than throwing away one's jewelry or burning the comics or smashing the TV set will make a bad boy or girl into a good one.

We've got to be new people before we can be good. We've got to be born again.

That's what Jesus told Nicodemus. Read about it in the next story.

## YOU CAN BE LIKE JESUS

One night when Jesus was praying on the Mount of Olives, he was interrupted by a visitor.

A very wealthy and influential teacher by the name of Nicodemus had come to talk to Him to find out who He was and what He planned to do. Nicodemus did not come to Jesus to find out how to be good. He felt he was good enough. He had been born a Jew, and all his life he had been very careful to do everything he was supposed to do, like washing all the way to his elbows before he ate.

He said to Jesus, "Rabbi, we know that Thou art a teacher sent from God: for no man can do these miracles that Thou doest, except God be with him."

Jesus smiled. He liked a compliment once in a while. But then He spoke seriously. "Except a man be born again, he cannot see the kingdom of God."

Nicodemus was taken by surprise. He had often said that the heathen were born again when they became Jews, but must a Jew be born again? Was Jesus suggesting that he was no better than a heathen? He said, "How can a man be born when he is old?"

Jesus didn't try to explain, and I'm glad He didn't. I'm sure we never could have understood. He said, "The wind blows wherever it wants to, and you can hear the sound, but you cannot tell where it comes from or where it goes to. That is the way it is when you are born of the Spirit." No one sees the Spirit of God come into our lives; no one knows how He works; but everyone can see the results, the kind expression on the face, the gentle, thoughtful deeds of the one who is born again.

But again Nicodemus asked, "How can these things be?"

Jesus still didn't explain. He never has. But He reminded Nicodemus of the time when the Children of Israel were marching through the wilderness and many of them sinned and were bitten by poisonous snakes. As they lay dying, Moses made a snake of brass and lifted it up on a pole; and everyone who looked at that brass serpent was cured. One of these days, Jesus told Nicodemus, the Son of man will be lifted up; and everyone who believes on Him will be saved. "For God so loved the world, that He gave His only-begotten Son, that whosoever believeth in Him should not perish, but have everlasting life."

How simple it is to be born again. Just look at Jesus and believe that He loves you. That's all we have to do.

You and I can't actually see Jesus. But we can read about Him, we can pray to Him, we can think about Him. And as we do these things, we shall become like Him. Think of being as kind as Jesus! as patient as Jesus! as obedient as Jesus! as thoughtful as He was!

You can be. Turn your eyes upon Him, think of Him always, remember that He loves you—and you will become like Him

## CAROLYN'S FATHER

Carolyn lay on her bed and looked up at the ceiling. In a few minutes she'd have to get ready for school.

She closed her eyes. "Please, God," she prayed, "make my father want to join the church and be baptized."

It wasn't the first morning Carolyn had prayed for her father. In the moment before she had to get up, she thought back over the many months of mornings when she had voiced that same prayer.

Carolyn's mother was a church member, and Father went to church—sometimes. But he had never been baptized and joined the church.

About three months before this an evangelist had come to the town where Carolyn lived. He had begun a series of revival meetings and had been preaching four nights a week ever since.

At the very beginning of the meetings Carolyn talked to her mother. "Let's ask Daddy to come to the meetings with us. Most of them will be at night, so his work won't interfere. If he comes, and if we pray for him, maybe he'll be converted."

Now the meetings were nearly over. "Just another two weeks," the evangelist had said last night. "Dear God," Carolyn whispered, "please hurry."

Then she glanced at the clock—and realized she'd better hurry, too, or she'd be late for school.

She dressed so quickly that she managed to spend a few minutes eating breakfast with Father.

"Daddy," she said, "would you do me a favor?"

He seemed to be in a good mood. "Sure." Carolyn and her dad nearly always got along well together.

"Daddy, please be baptized and join the church."

Oh, dear! She hadn't meant to be so blunt.

The smile disappeared from Father's face. "I have explained to you and Mother again and again, I am not going to join the church. Religion is good for women and girls, not for men. Please don't ask me again."

Carolyn felt so bad she couldn't eat any more. She was glad Daddy had to leave for work right away, because she felt like crying.

Of course she had to go to school, no matter how she felt. But worse was in store.

On the way to school she met Barbara, her best friend. It just so happened that Barbara's father also was not a baptized church member. Both girls were in the sixth grade. They were not baptized either. They had agreed to try to work it so that they would be baptized together with their fathers—the four of them at once.

As Carolyn walked to school this morning she met Barbara in the usual place. Barbara was radiantly happy.

She exclaimed, "The best thing happened! You'll never believe it. But last night the evangelist visited my father, and Daddy agreed to join the church. I feel so good today."

"That's wonderful." Carolyn tried to be cheerful, but it hurt. If only her own father would say the same!

"There is more," Barbara went on. "I'm going to be baptized with him tomorrow night."

Carolyn stared at her. "What about our plan to be baptized together?"

"Well, I thought about that, but the minister said it would be better if I didn't wait."

Carolyn isn't sure to this day what happened the rest of the way to school. It seemed as if the bottom had dropped out of everything.

She hardly heard a thing the teacher said all day. Many times she prayed within herself. What had she been doing wrong? Why didn't God answer? What could she do now? She resolved that she would be more agreeable than ever before at home, more pleasant, more willing to do what her mother and father asked of her. Then maybe, she reasoned, Father might see that it was a good thing to be a Christian, and he might change his mind.

The final two weeks of the evangelistic series came to an end. On the last Sunday night, Daddy said he was too busy to attend. Carolyn went with Mother.

The evangelist preached a wonderful sermon. At the end he made a very serious appeal. "Those of you who have been thinking of giving your lives to God, don't put it off any longer. On Wednesday night we will have our last meeting. At the conclusion of that meeting there will be a baptism. And that will be the last. I don't know when there will be another. So all of you who have never been baptized, I urge you to come down to the front right now and give yourselves to Jesus."

Carolyn heard. She had hoped to be baptized with Barbara—and that hadn't worked out. She had hoped so very much to be baptized with her father—and that wasn't going to work out. She had waited as long as she could. She walked down to the front—alone.

Perhaps, if she led the way, her daddy would follow her. She hoped so.

On Wednesday night she went to church with a paper bag that had the clothing in it the preacher had told her to bring so she would have something dry to wear after the baptism. Mother was with her. But not Father. He wasn't even going to be there to see her baptized. At the last minute his foreman had told him he'd have to work overtime.

Carolyn sat at the front with the others who were to be baptized. But she didn't listen to the sermon. She was thinking, "There is still time. Daddy could change his mind even now and be baptized. He could come in that back door during the sermon. Please, dear God, make my father come."

But the clock went round to nine o'clock, the time when the preacher always closed his sermons, and Daddy hadn't come.

The preacher had finished his sermon. Carolyn could tell, even though she hadn't listened very well.

And then, strange to tell, the preacher went on preaching. It sounded a bit as if he was making up his talk as he went along. About ten past nine, Carolyn thought she saw him looking anxiously at the back door. And a few minutes later, he looked at that door in the same way again.

"Is he expecting someone to come?" she thought. "Please, Jesus, make it be my daddy!"

At nine fifteen she saw a marvelous smile spread over the preacher's face. She turned around—and there, coming in the back door, was Father! He had a paper bag under his arm, just like Carolyn's, and he didn't stop back there where Mother was. He came all the way down to the front. He tapped Carolyn on the shoulder and whispered, "Move over a little bit, dear, and let me sit beside you."

Minutes later Carolyn's prayers were answered. She and Father were baptized—together!

## FIVE GOOD EXCUSES

The man was sick—paralyzed, in fact, so that he had to stay in bed all the time—and that is the first good excuse he had for not going to church. You could hardly require a sick man to get up from his bed to go to church, could you?

But it just so happened that this young man wanted to go—so badly, in fact, that he persuaded four of his friends to put him on a stretcher and carry him there.

He had heard that Jesus had come to town, and that He was speaking in a certain house. "Please take me to it," he begged.

His friends agreed. But when they reached the house, they found it full. Every seat was taken, people were even standing so thick in the doorway it was impossible for any more to enter.

That was the second good excuse he had for not attending church. You wouldn't require a man to attend church if, when he got there, there wasn't room enough to get in? But this man persisted.

"It's impossible," his friends said.

"Unless," he must have answered them, "you take me up onto the roof and let me down through the ceiling."

Did you ever try to hoist a man on a stretcher up onto a roof? It would be exceedingly dangerous.

That's the third good excuse that man had. Surely you wouldn't expect a man to risk all the dangers of being pulled up onto a roof just to attend church.

"Lift me up there," he said. "I don't mind if it's dangerous. Jesus is in there, and that's where I want to be."

They didn't have any ropes, and they would need several. That was the fourth good excuse.

One or two of the friends left to see if they couldn't find some. I suppose the others stayed to keep the sick man company.

At last the men came back. No doubt they tied a rope around the man to keep him on the stretcher, and then began the very difficult job of lifting him.

Can you see them? One man climbs the outside stairway and gets a firm foothold behind the low wall that runs around the edge of the flat roof. He lets the ropes down, and the three friends tie them to the four corners of the stretcher. Then they climb the stairs, and each one takes a rope and pulls. But they must pull evenly, or one corner will be higher than the others and the stretcher will tip. Their arms grow weary, but they dare not let go.

At last the man is up there. They must make a hole in the roof. What will the owner say? He'll be angry, without any question, and raise a fuss.

So that was the fifth good excuse that sick man had. "Tear up the roof," he said. "I'll talk to the owner later."

The friends tore open a large hole and let the man down in front of Jesus. Jesus saw their faith and forgave the man his sins and healed him of his disease, so that he stood up, picked up his stretcher, and walked out of the house in front of them all, completely well.

He had five good excuses for not going to church that day. But wasn't it a good thing he went!

## THINGS TO COME

When you watch the news on TV, or when you read in the newspapers about hydrogen bombs and inter-continental missiles, do you ever wonder what is going to happen to the world?

Unfortunately, none of us can see very far into the future. On Friday morning, November 22, 1963, how many people knew that President John F. Kennedy would be shot to death that very afternoon? No one did. Not even the man who was about to kill him. He couldn't be sure he wouldn't miss. When we talk about things that are going to happen in the future, the best any of us can do is guess.

But God is different. He knows the end from the beginning. He can talk about things that haven't happened yet as if they had already taken place.

And He has told us in the Bible that the world is coming to an end.

So that we would be sure this was true, He told us through the prophet Daniel that just before the end of the world "many shall run to and fro, and knowledge shall be increased."

In Daniel's day, 2,500 years ago, men traveled on horses or camels, and most of them never traveled at all. It was like this until about sixty-five years ago. Daniel prophesied that a time would come when many people would travel to and fro and that they would do so at great speed. Now, at last, that very thing is happening. Everyone is on the go—in automobiles, jet airplanes, and rockets.

Knowledge has been increased, too, in our days. We know so very much more about chemistry and physics and medicine now than people did in Daniel's day, don't we? In the last twenty or thirty years, men have learned more about the world around us than mankind discovered in all the ages of the past.

Remember, Daniel wrote that all these things would happen in "the time of the end." Apparently the world is coming to an end.

The apostle Paul said, "In the last days perilous times shall come. For men shall be lovers of their own selves, covetous, boasters, proud, blasphemers, disobedient to parents, unthankful, unholy."

All we have to do is to glance at the front page of a newspaper to see that this prophecy is being fulfilled. Criminals steal and murder more than ever, teenagers fight gang wars, law-abiding citizens fear to walk outside at night lest they be set upon and beaten, and statesmen and government leaders threaten to destroy the whole world with hydrogen bombs and poisonous bacteria. We are living in perilous times, aren't we?

Paul said that these dangerous days would be the days before the end. "This know also," he said, "that in the last days perilous times shall come."

So both Paul and Daniel agree that the world is coming to an end. Jesus Himself said the very same thing. The disciples asked Him once, "What shall be the sign . . . of the end of the world?"

Jesus answered, "This gospel of the kingdom shall be preached in all the world for a witness unto all nations; and then shall the end come."

Never before have so many ministers and missionaries been preaching about Christ. When Jesus spoke to His disciples that day, there weren't more than a handful of Christians in the world, and all of them were in Palestine. Nowadays there are millions of Christians, and they live in every country around the globe. The gospel of the kingdom of Christ is being preached everywhere, as Jesus said it would be. And He said, "Then shall the end come."

The world will not be destroyed by hydrogen bombs. Don't be afraid of that. When Jesus talked about the end of the world, He meant the day when He would come back to the earth. We don't know when it will be. We know it will be soon.

Jesus said that we will "see the Son of man coming in the clouds of heaven with power and great glory." He will "send His angels with a great sound of a trumpet, and they shall gather together His elect from the four winds, from one end of heaven to the other."

Paul wrote, "The Lord Himself shall descend from heaven with a shout, with the voice of the Archangel, and with the trump of God: and the dead in Christ shall rise first: then we which are alive and remain shall be caught up together with them in the clouds, to meet the Lord in the air: and so shall we ever be with the Lord."

A small black cloud will appear in the east about half the size of a man's hand.

As the cloud draws closer, it grows larger and glows like fire. The air seems filled with angels. Jesus sits on a throne in the midst of the cloud, a crown of glory resting on His brow, and His face shining brighter than the sun.

The angels have been singing. Now they stop, and there is a great silence broken only by the cries of evil men who are calling for the rocks and mountains to fall on them and hide them from the face of Him who sits on the throne.

Even, for a moment, the righteous fear. They have always worshiped and respected God, but they never realized He was so powerful as this.

Then Jesus, knowing they are afraid, smiles on them and says, "My grace is sufficient for you." Their faces light up, and joy fills their hearts.

Jesus calls the righteous dead to waken. All who died loving and serving God now come forth from their graves, and angels sweep down to pick them up and carry them to the cloud.

Then the living righteous are caught up and borne to the cloud, too, to be forever with the Lord.

And that is the beginning of the good things the future holds for all who give their hearts and lives to God.

If you would like to read where the Bible says these things, look in Isaiah 46:10; Daniel 12:4; Matthew 24:6, 7, 30, 31, 33; 2 Timothy 3:1–5; Revelation 6:14–17; 14:14–20; 19:11–16; 1 Thessalonians 4:16, 17.

## YOUR WONDERFUL FUTURE

When all the good people are on the cloud with Jesus, they will begin the great journey to heaven.

On the cloud are all who are safe to save—all who ever lived who loved God enough to obey Him.

Some of them lived thousands of years ago. Here are Adam and Eve, the first man and woman on earth, and their son, Abel, who was killed by his brother because he obeyed God.

Here, too, are David and Abraham and Joseph, and the great prophets Isaiah and Jeremiah and Daniel, and the apostles Paul and Peter and John. And besides them, there is a crowd so great that no one can number them.

Most have been sleeping in their graves since they died, waiting for the resurrection. Now Jesus has come. Their graves have been opened. They have come forth. Their bodies have been changed. Sickness and suffering are ended forever.

But some of the people on the cloud with Jesus never died. They are the faithful who were alive when He came. You may be among them. For Jesus will return so soon that you will probably see Him come.

All the people who are not safe to save—those who think it is all right to disobey God once in a while, or who think it isn't really necessary to keep all the Ten Commandments—will be left behind, dead.

The good people on the cloud fly up through space, past the sun and the stars, out beyond the boundaries of our Milky Way, on, past galaxies and nebulas, to heaven, the home of God. There they will live 1,000 years.

It will be really living. No more aches and pains, no more colds and headaches, no more sore tonsils, no more hospitals, no more hard tests, no more baffling problems and bad grades. Your mind will be clear, your muscles will be strong and vigorous, you will have unlimited energy, and you will live like this forever.

When the thousand years are over, Christ will call the righteous together, and they will return to the earth. This time they will not travel on a cloud, but in the royal city, which the Bible calls the New Jerusalem. It is a city like none we have ever seen and is described in Revelation 21 and 22. John the apostle saw it in a vision. He wrote, "I John saw the Holy City, New Jerusalem, coming down from God out of heaven."

At that time God will make the world all over new. John saw him doing it, and he said, "I saw a new heaven and a new earth: for the first heaven and the first earth were passed away."

In the Bible you can find many descriptions of the new earth. It will be a fabulous place to live.

"The eyes of the blind shall be opened, and the ears of the deaf shall be unstopped. Then shall the lame man leap as an hart, and the tongue of the dumb sing: for in the wilderness shall waters break out, and streams in the desert."

"And the ransomed of the Lord shall return, and come to Zion with songs and everlasting joy upon their heads: they shall obtain joy and gladness, and sorrow and sighing shall flee away."

"The wolf also shall dwell with the lamb, and the leopard shall lie down with the kid; and the calf and the young lion and the fatling together; and a little child shall lead them."

"They shall not hurt nor destroy in all My holy mountain: for the earth shall be full of the knowledge of the Lord, as the waters cover the sea."

"And God shall wipe away all tears from their eyes; and there shall be no more death, neither sorrow, nor crying, neither shall there be any more pain: for the former things are passed away."

God invites you to live in the new earth. This is the future He is planning for you.

There you will see your dreams fulfilled. You will reach your highest ambitions.

Do you want to be a scientist, probing into the secrets of nature? In heaven you will have Him who designed all nature as your Teacher. Christ the Creator will explain to you the mysteries of things He Himself made. With such a Teacher, you will soon know more science than the greatest scientists earth has ever known, and still Christ will teach you more.

Do you want to be rich, to have a large house and a big estate? Jesus told His disciples, "In My Father's house are many mansions....I go to prepare a place for you." You will have houses and lands! Do you love animals? Do you wish you had a dog, a cat, a horse? They are waiting for you.

Do you want to be a doctor or a nurse? Do you want to study all about the brain and the heart and muscles and nerves? how they are made and how they work? There will be no sick people for you to heal in heaven. But Jesus Christ Himself, who made man in the beginning, will be there to tell you all about the human body. He will explain to you the deep mysteries of life, secrets that no one on earth could teach you now.

Do you aspire to politics? Would you like to be a Congressman or a Senator, perhaps the President of your country or a judge of the Supreme Court? Perhaps you don't have a chance in this life. But in heaven the good people will sit on thrones as kings and will judge angels. If you are faithful to Jesus, you will sit beside Him on His throne. He says so. Read about it in Revelation 3:21.

Would you like to be an airplane pilot? Would you like to man a rocket, or be an astronaut and go to the moon or Mars? Angels fly through space without need for airplanes, rockets, or capsules—and so will you. It is one of the thrills in the future God has planned for you.

Do you just want to be with Jesus? Do you long to sit beside Him and talk to Him and tell Him you love Him and appreciate what He has done for you? In heaven you can. You will see Jesus face to face; you will talk to Him as to your very best friend.

This is heaven. And still there is more. For "eye hath not seen, nor ear heard, neither have entered into the heart of man, the things which God hath prepared for them that love Him."

We can only dream of the most wonderful things we can imagine; and after we have let our minds go wild, as it were, and we have dreamed of utter impossibilities, then we must know that heaven is even better than that.

And it is yours. This is your wonderful future. All God asks of you in return is that you love Him. He says, "My son, My daughter, give Me your heart." Bow your head right now, won't you, and tell Him that you will.

# OUTNUMBERED!

The noise was so slight that only a trained ear could have heard it. It lasted only a moment, and then it was gone, and the engines of the big Air Force bomber sounded as sweet and smooth as they always had.

But, Mac, the flight engineer, had a trained ear, and he heard the noise. His heart missed a beat, and he glanced around at the other crew members. Apparently they hadn't heard it, not even the captain.

Mac glanced out the cockpit window. The Pacific Ocean stretched clear to the horizon. There were, he knew, some islands just beyond the horizon, over to the southwest, but they were South Sea Islands, and he remembered stories he'd heard as a boy. Many of the people were cannibals. They ate strangers.

The plane droned on. The navigator had worked out the course long ago and was now reading a paperback. The pilot had put the controls on automatic, and he and the copilot were dozing, their heads against their headrests, their eyes closed.

Back through the fuselage were gunners at the gun positions, as relaxed as the men in the cockpit. They weren't concerned, Mac thought. Why should he be?

The noise came again. A little louder this time, and it hung on just a little longer. The navigator didn't notice it, the copilot still dozed, but when Mac looked at the captain, their eyes met. Only for an instant, but it was long enough to confirm Mac's fears. He had not imagined the noise. Something was wrong with one of the engines.

Sooner than before, the noise came again, and then it came so often and with increasing loudness so that everyone heard it.

Tension crackled in the cockpit. The navigator slammed his paperback and Mac checked the dials. One was flickering in the danger zone. He ran through all the routine procedures for correcting the defect, but none helped. The copilot grabbed the engine manual, reading off instructions so Mac wouldn't miss any.

The engine got so bad the pilot cut it and feathered the propeller. The trouble spread to the next engine, and from there to a third. The bomber was losing altitude.

Mac strained his eyes for a glimpse of one of those islands. The navigator noticed and shook his head. "Nearest island is a hundred miles away, Mac."

"Prepare to ditch!" But the captain's order wasn't necessary. The crew had already prepared.

The plane made a remarkably smooth landing, and the men had plenty of time to inflate the life raft and stock it with emergency supplies. They were all safely aboard and well away from the plane when it sank.

They rigged a sail, and the navigator set a course for the nearest island; but mostly they went where the wind blew them.

"What's the use of landing?" Mac said. "We'll only run into the the savages. They'll either kill us or turn us over to the enemy. There are enemy garrisons on all these islands."

"There have been missionaries on these islands," the copilot said.

"Missionaries!" Mac scoffed. "Missionaries can't change cannibals."

After two and a half days the men saw land low on the horizon. Under cover of darkness they went ashore, hoping to remain hidden until they could work out some way to get back to the American forces.

They set up camp in a protected spot, and Mac grinned. "No one will find us here."

For several days no one did find them. And then one afternoon Mac heard a rustle behind him and looked around. An islander was staring at him. A moment later the man disappeared.

But the captain had seen him before he vanished. "It's only a matter of time now," he commented. "That man will return, and he will not come alone."

"We will be outnumbered for sure, but at least we can go down fighting." The tail gunner caressed his service pistol.

The copilot smiled. "Have you forgotten that there have been missionaries on these islands? These people may have been converted."

Mac snorted in derision. The copilot was always talking about those missionaries. But though Mac snorted, he didn't say anything. For the first time he realized that their only hope for getting out of this spot alive lay, not in the tail gunner's service pistol, but on the slim chance that these islanders had indeed been converted.

The sun swung around to the west and dropped rapidly toward the horizon. The sky was rosy red and purple and gold. The next minute it was dark. The men waited.

Then there was a light, the flickering flame of a burning torch held in the powerful hand of a South Sea Islander. The light reflected off the swarthy bodies of a long line of huge men coming rapidly toward the American camp.

The tail gunner fingered his pistol. The captain raised a hand. "Hold your fire. These men are not armed."

And now the man with the torch had reached the edge of the airmen's camp. He stopped. He walked forward slowly. He handed one of the airmen a black book—a Bible!

Mac glanced at the copilot. Maybe the missionaries

But he didn't have time to think about the missionaries just then. Several more of the islanders came into the clearing carrying food and drink!

And when those good things had been taken care of, the leader opened the Bible and read a passage that even Mac recognized. Then the islanders began singing. Mac couldn't catch all the words, but he remembered the tunes. He had sung them in Sunday School back in Christian America. They were the same songs exactly!

To make a long story short, the airmen remained on the island eighty-seven more days. Every evening the islanders came with food and read the Bible to the men and sang hymns. More than two hundred of them knew the Americans were there, but never a word of their presence was breathed to the enemy.

At last the islanders helped the airmen construct a raft on which, in the dead of night, the Americans set sail. After a few days they were picked up by one of their own Air Force planes.

In a hospital recuperating from the experience, Mac spoke for the whole group.

"You can tell the world that I am now a devout Christian," he said. "Those islanders gave us the Bible, and they led us Christians to Christ. Thank God for missionaries."

# WALKING INTO THE SEA

Stew, who was the worst drinker on the ship, turned in his bunk and reached out a hand toward the table nearby. But there was nothing on it.

"Where's that bottle?" he roared. He swung his feet onto the floor and gazed angrily at the empty table. "Who took my bottle?" he shouted louder than the first time, but no one heard him.

For much of his life Stew had drunk heavily, and at last his mind had given way. For several days now he had been seeing things—snakes slithering around under the bunk, big black hairy spiders running up and down his body.

The other sailors on the ship had shut him up in one of the rooms. Now he was feeling a bit better, and he wanted a drink. "Who's got my bottle?" he bellowed.

He staggered to the porthole. "Look at that!" he exclaimed thickly. "We're in port, and there's the little boat that will take us to land. I'll go and buy myself another bottle, and no one will take it from me. Better get my things, though, so I can stay a day or two and have a real good time."

He got his bag. By some mistake the door had been left unlocked. Stew stumbled down the corridor and up to the deck.

"Ahoy there, mates!" he shouted. "Let down the rope ladder. I'm going ashore."

A sailor came over. "What's gotten into you, Stew? We're out in the middle of the Pacific Ocean. You can't go ashore."

"We're in port, and I'm going ashore," said Stew. "Don't argue with me. I know what I want to do; and just because you guys take my bottles away, you don't need to think you can keep me from going ashore and buying more. Let that rope down!"

The sailor was about to say something else when two other sailors ran up, their eyes twinkling. They winked at the first sailor and said, "Stew, you want the rope ladder put down, do you? We'll be glad to do that for you."

They put the ladder over the side, and quite a crowd of sailors gathered around. Life got pretty boring in the middle of the ocean, and this promised to be fun.

"What will you do when you get to the bottom of the ladder, Stew?" someone shouted.

"Get into the little boat down there and go to shore!" said Stew. "Now help me onto the ladder."

Many hands reached forward to help. And Stew needed them! Even when he was on the ladder he could hardly hold the rope. Just how he was able to hold on to the ladder and keep a grip on his bag I do not know, but down the ship's side he went.

Some of the sailors were worried. "Surely he knows there is no little boat," they said.

But when Stew reached the bottom of the ladder, he stepped out onto the boat. Except that, of course, there was no boat there; so he walked into the sea instead! He went under at once, and he came up several yards away.

"Man overboard!" the sailors shouted.

Immediately bells rang. The ship's engines stopped. A boat was lowered, and Stew was hauled to safety.

"Did that really happen?" I asked the storyteller.

"Yes," he said, "I was one of the sailors who watched."

"Well," I said, "drink surely does make people do the silliest things!"

# PUP ON A BIKE

"I'm going to wear my pink orlon. Pink's Bob's favorite color, and he always says I look my best dressed in pink."

"Well, I'm going to wear my green skirt with that heavenly blouse Dad gave me a couple of weeks ago. You really must stop by the house and see it. But I haven't decided yet whether I ought to go in my pale blue dress. It matches my eyes just perfectly, but I know Dad will want me to wear that blouse—and I don't know which colors Ed prefers. I haven't known him as long as you've known Bob."

So Frances and Evelyn chattered gaily through the streets of Pasadena, California, not so very long ago. Comparing dresses, comparing boyfriends, planning a party. A very pleasant day.

But the same day that was so satisfactory for them was filled with tragedy for a certain little seven-year-old.

For weeks Billy had wanted a dog. He had begged and pleaded and coaxed and entreated. At last his parents had said that if someone would give him a dog he could have it.

And now, joy of joys, one of his friends had given him a little pup.

But there was a problem Billy hadn't thought of. How to get the puppy home? He had ridden to his friend's house on his bicycle.

He picked up the pup and climbed on the bicycle and headed homeward. But he hadn't gone far before the pup wiggled out of his hand and ran under a bush.

Billy "heeled the bike over to the bush and reached for the pup. The pup nuzzled his outstretched fingers and ran back a couple of yards. Billy pulled the bike after him, reached out for the pup, and again the little dog ran away.

Billy caught it at last, in both hands. But how could he control the bike and keep two hands around the pup?

Impossible for a seven-year-old. He let go one hand—and the dog wiggled free.

How often this sort of thing happened I do not know. But soon poor little Billy could take it no more. He was tired, he was hungry, he was all alone.

He dropped the bike, sat down on the curb with the pup in his arms, and wept.

And just about that time Frances and Evelyn came around the corner. "…fun to go to parties," Frances was saying, "when the right boys—" She stopped. "Evelyn, what's wrong with that little fellow?"

"Let's ask him," Evelyn said.

"Little boy," Frances said gently, "can we help you?"

A tear-stained face looked up. "The puppy always gets away from me," the little boy sobbed, "and I can't ride the bike and hold him too, and Mommy's going to be worried 'cause I'm not home yet, and I'm hungry, and the little puppy always wiggles out of my hands when I try to ride, and I can't leave the bike here, and there's no one to help me."

The tears came again.

"Well, now," said Frances, "that sounds like a lot of troubles. Tell us your telephone number. We'll call your mother, and she'll come and get you."

"We don't have a telephone, and I'm never going to be able to get home with the puppy and the bike."

"Cheer up," Frances said. "We'll ask the policeman to help you."

Quickly Frances and Evelyn ran down the street and over a block and reported the problem. Immediately a radio message went out, and Frances and Evelyn, hurrying back, were just in time to see two kind and understanding officers hoisting a teeny bike and a little pup and a very small boy into the squad car. The face that had been so sad was wreathed in smiles. The puppy was licking the tears away.

"Boyfriends and parties," Evelyn sighed. "It's been a good day."

"But helping little boys with puppy dogs," said Frances, "was the best part of all."

# ANGELS WITH SHOVELS

Snow had been falling all day. It had covered the walk leading up to Mrs. Hilton's front door, and by now the wind had piled it up in a great heap against her back door.

Mrs. Hilton looked at it all in dismay. She wasn't as young as she used to be. Her husband had died some years back. Her children were grown up and had gone away. She lived alone, and shoveling snow was too much for her.

Two or three times during the day she saw Bill and Jack, the two boys who lived next door, come out and clear the snow from their walks. She almost called to them to ask them to come and do hers, but she stopped herself. Of course they would want to be paid. All boys wanted to be paid nowadays. And she couldn't afford to pay.

Once, just as night was falling, she noticed Bill and Jack leaning on their shovels and looking over toward her house, but then they turned and went indoors.

Mrs. Hilton went to bed early. There's not much for an elderly lady to do in the evening, especially when she's snow-bound. "I'll need a good sleep anyway," Mrs. Hilton reasoned, "with all that snow to move in the morning."

Just before midnight she awakened and looked out the window. The snow was still falling, but more gently now, and it seemed as if the storm was blowing itself out. The world was

white and beautiful and wonderfully silent, and the light from the streetlamps sparkled on the snowy crystals.

Then she remembered the sidewalks she had to clear in the morning and sighed.

It was hard being old and weak.

She dozed off again.

Hark! What was that?

Voices under the window! The sound of metal scraping against concrete!

Mrs. Hilton lay on her bed too frightened to move. But she must see what was going on. And something about the voices sounded strangely familiar.

She slipped out of bed and peeked through the window around the edge of the blind.

The storm was over. The sun was just coming up, all red and orange against a clear blue sky. And Bill and Jack were shoveling snow from Mrs. Hilton's walks!

"Those dear, blessed boys," she whispered. "I must get out my purse and find some money for them. But I suppose I'd better put some more clothes on before I go to the door."

The boys, working hard, were quicker than Mrs. Hilton. They finished the front walk and went around and did the back. Mrs. Hilton checked on them once more, out another window, and saw they had finished. Not a flake of snow remained on any of her walks.

"Now they'll be knocking on the door and asking for their pay," she thought.

She rushed to the door, opened it—and saw the boys running home.

"Boys," she called, "come back and I'll pay you."

"Oh, no," they shouted. "We couldn't take any money for a little job like that."

Mrs. Hilton just stood and stared. Surely she had been visited by angels with shovels. Were there really boys who would do a job just for kindness and then refuse to be paid for it?

Suddenly it broke through her mind that it was really so!

She swung around, reached for the phone, and called the boys' mother and told her what had happened. Then she sat down and wrote a letter to the editor of a newspaper. He printed the letter, and the kind deed those boys did that morning has been read about all around the world. And I am sure the angels have repeated the story all through heaven too.

Doing kind things without being paid is, after all, what Jesus did for us when He came to earth so long ago.

## "JESUS, NEW YORK 8"

The clerk in the New York City post office looked at the card and blinked. He had never seen a piece of mail addressed like this before.

The words were scraggly. "Written by a child," the clerk reasoned. He read the address again: "Jesus, New York 8."

Suddenly his right arm stretched out, and that postcard sailed through the air. It came to rest in a mail sack—the very mail sack that the boy who mailed the card wanted it put into.

Behind that postcard is a story that the post office clerk will probably never know. This is it:

The boy who wrote the card is named Garry. Garry was a very active fellow who loved to play baseball and basketball; and there was nothing he enjoyed more than camping.

One weekend when he was eleven, he and a friend went camping together, and Garry came home sick.

Mother called the doctor, and the doctor put Garry in the hospital. He said Garry had polio. He had to lie in an iron lung for several months, because he couldn't breathe by himself. The doctors thought surely he was going to die.

But Garry lived. The fever went down, and he could breathe on his own again. He was allowed to go home. But he couldn't walk. He had to sit in a wheelchair all day, and the doctor said it would probably be that way for the rest of his life. Again and again he asked himself, Why did God let this happen to me?

One day, when he was feeling particularly discouraged, his mother wheeled him in front of the television and turned the set on. Garry didn't want to watch television just then. He wanted to stare out the window and feel miserable.

But when the picture on the screen came into focus, Garry saw a boy in a wheelchair talking to a minister. Garry was interested now! The boy's mother was saying to the preacher, "Why did God let my son get hurt like this?"

The very question Garry had been asking!

He listened closely, and the preacher explained that God does not bring suffering into the world. It is Satan, God's enemy, who makes people suffer. God tries to make people happy. When pain and sickness come, God does not desert us. He is not punishing us. He comes very close to us when we are ill, and He wants us to remember that He loves us still.

The more the preacher talked, the happier Garry felt, and when the program came to an end he said, "Mom, I'm going to watch again next week."

Garry and his mother watched again and again. It became quite a habit with them. Garry especially liked the stories that the speaker, Pastor Fagal, told about Jesus. He began to see that even if he did have to sit in a wheelchair all the time, he could still live a useful life with Jesus helping him.

In every program the announcer talked about a Bible correspondence course and urged everyone to send for it. "There's even one for you younger folk," he said. "You'll love it. It tells all about Jesus. To enroll, just send us a postcard and we'll send you the lessons absolutely free. Our address is 'Faith for Today, Box 8, New York, New York 10008.' "

One day Garry decided he wanted that course. He pushed his wheelchair over to a drawer where postcards and pencils were kept, and he rummaged around. Yes, here was a pencil and—ah, yes, here was a postcard.

He wrote on the "message" side that he would like the junior course. Then he turned the card over to write the address.

But, oh, dear! He had forgotten it. He couldn't even remember the name of the program. His mind had been playing tricks on him like this ever since he got sick. Mother wasn't home right then; so he couldn't ask her. He couldn't think of the name of the man who talked. And what was the city? New York? Yes, it seemed the man had said New York several times. Must be New York.

Garry wrote New York. But surely there ought to be a box number, or a zip code, or something. New York was a big place. The man said "8" several times. Was that the box number or the zip code? Garry decided it must be the zip, although it didn't seem long enough. He wrote 8 after New York.

So far, so good—maybe. But even New York 8 would hardly be enough. If only he could remember the name of the program.

Then he thought of something. The man had said the lessons were all about Jesus. "Perhaps," thought Garry, "if I send this to Jesus, it will get to the right place."

And that's how the postcard turned up in the New York City post office addressed to "Jesus, New York 8."

There is a story I would like the post office clerk to tell me. How was it that he knew to put the postcard in the Faith for Today mail sack—right where Garry wanted it to go?

Could it be that the clerk had watched the TV program? Could it be that the message and people on the program were so much like Jesus that when he thought of Jesus he thought of Faith for Today? I like to think that was the reason.

Tell me, if a postcard came to your town addressed to Jesus, would the mailman bring it to your house?

## BOY GOD HONORED

Did you ever dream that you were standing beside an apple tree loaded with ripe apples? You reached out to pick one—and the apple tree disappeared.

Or were you selling magazines, and all the time you were talking to a customer, you were sure he was going to buy; then just when you expected him to put his hand in his pocket and take out some money he said No and walked away?

If you have ever had an experience like these, you know how Kirkland felt a while ago.

The thing Kirkland wanted more than anything else in the world was to go to college. He had been planning on it ever since he was in grade school. He had studied hard all through elementary school and high school. Always he had done well.

Now, at last, he had almost reached his goal. Kirkland does not live in the United States, and in his country it is very important for a high school student to pass a certain examination if he wants to go to college.

Kirkland was ready to take that highly important exam. Then, just one week before the exam, his teacher announced, "The examination will be next Saturday."

That presented no particular problem to most of the boys. But Kirkland had been brought up to obey what the Bible says. He knew that back there in Exodus, chapter twenty, the fourth commandment reads, "Remember the Sabbath day, to keep it holy. Six days shalt thou labor, and do all thy work: but the seventh day is the Sabbath of the Lord thy God: in it thou shalt not do any work."

The seventh day, of course, is Saturday. Kirkland knew it wouldn't be right for him to take that test on God's Sabbath.

For a moment he felt as if he had been hit over the head with a hammer. If he didn't take the test, he would never be allowed to enter college. All his hopes would come to a sudden, crushing stop. And then hope returned. Surely the examination would not be given on Saturday only. There would be another day when students could take it.

After class he went up to the teacher and explained that he could not take the exam on Saturday. It would be against his conscience.

"Nonsense!" the teacher exclaimed. "Of course you can take the exam on Saturday. Everyone else can; you can too."

That was that. The teacher left, and Kirkland walked home in despair.

Would God help him? Heaven's help was his only hope. He prayed that night, and the next morning he went to school hoping the teacher would tell him he could take the test at another time. But the teacher said nothing about it.

Kirkland prayed on Tuesday night. How he prayed! And on Wednesday he talked to the teacher again.

The teacher responded the same way he had the first time. "Ridiculous!" he snorted. "I never heard anything so foolish in my life."

"But, sir, I cannot come on Saturday. It is God's Sabbath, and I go to church then."

The teacher looked at him. "Tell me, boy, would you rather take this examination on Saturday and maybe win a scholarship to college, or attend church and miss all chance?"

"Sir," said Kirkland, "I would rather go to church." The teacher waved a hand in disgust, and Kirkland knew the conversation was over. What should he do? It was so very importaut to pass this examination. Perhaps it would be all right to take it on Sabbath, just this once.

Kirkland put that idea out of his mind, and in the evening he went to prayer meeting. There he had the happiest surprise of his life.

The pastor said, "Kirkland, your teacher got in touch with me today. He asked me whether it really was necessary for you to go to church on Saturday. Of course I told him it was. I really believe he wanted to work out some way for you to take the test.

"I explained to him how the Bible says that the Sabbath starts at sunset on Friday evening and ends at sunset on Saturday evening. He was surprised at that, so I pulled out my Bible (I had it with me just in case), and read him that text—"

Kirkland interrupted. "I know. You must mean, er, Leviticus 23:32, isn't it? 'From even unto even, shall ye celebrate your Sabbath.'"

"Good for you, Kirkland," the pastor said. "Well, when I read that to the teacher, I saw his eyes light up. 'Do you mean to tell me,' he said, 'that if the boy took the test after sunset it would be all right—though it would still be Saturday?'

"'That's right,' I said.

"'Then I'll tell you what to do,' he said. 'Go and see the chief inspector of education. He happens to be visiting the school today. Tell him what you've told me, and I think we can arrange something.'

"And so, Kirkland, to make a long story short, I went to see the inspector, and I have good news for you. You must stay with me all day Saturday; you must not be out of my sight for a moment. But then, after sunset, you may take the test."

That is how it all turned out, and Kirkland passed! Once again, when a boy honored God, God honored him.

# THE MYSTERY OF MR. MOORE'S GRAPES

I wish I knew what birds think about in their little minds. I wish I understood their language.

Because I would love to have a bird from Perth, Australia, come and tell me about Mr. Moore's grapes.

There is something very special about those grapes, as I will show you in a moment.

Now, I can understand part of the mystery. But I wish someone would tell me what the birds knew. That part of the mystery is too deep for me.

Did the birds know why they did what they did? Did they know the grapes were special? Did an angel tell them about Mr. Moore? Or could it possibly be that they didn't even see the grapes, that they didn't know they were there?

This last explanation seems fantastic, however, for the birds lived right beside Mr. Moore's grapes and flew past them every day.

But maybe I ought to tell you what it was that happened to the grapes, and something about Mr. Moore, and then perhaps you can tell me the answers.

Mr. H. N. Moore is a faithful Christian who lives in Perth, Australia. Perth is one of the largest cities of Australia, far over on the western side of the country.

Mr. Moore likes grapes, and they grow well in his part of the world. But the birds like grapes too. And since they don't care too much about the flavor, they manage to eat most of the grapes before they are ripe enough for the residents of Perth to enjoy. In fact, it is quite common for the birds to ruin three quarters of all the grapes that grow on Perthian vines.

By all appearances, Mr. Moore should never get more than a handful of grapes from his grapevines. For not only do birds from other parts of town fly frequently into his backyard, but many birds build their nests there. They make homes in trees right beside his house. Anytime Mr. Moore looks out he can see birds hunting beside his flower plants or singing in his shrubs.

A neighbor a few doors down the street grows grapes too. Recently he told Mr. Moore that the birds, with the help of the bees, had ruined all of his grapes. Not just three quarters of them. All of them.

But now we come to the remarkable thing I want to tell you about. In the spring not long ago Mr. Moore noticed that bunches were forming on his vines, and he went out and counted them. There turned out to be 108 of those little green bunches. A few months later, when the grapes were ripe, he counted the bunches again to see how many the birds had left. There were 108. Every one of his 108 bunches was still intact; not one of them was damaged. They were big, full, delicious bunches that reached almost to his elbow when he held them in his hand. Remember, the birds were thick in his yard all season. They completely destroyed all of his neighbor's grapes—but didn't harm one of his.

Can you explain this mystery? I can explain part of it, because I know that Mr. Moore pays tithe faithfully. He always takes one tenth of the money he earns and gives it back to God, and God has made a special promise to tithe payers. You can read it in Malachi 3:10, 11: "Bring ye all the tithes into the storehouse,...and prove me now herewith, saith the Lord of hosts, if I will not open you the windows of heaven, and pour you out a blessing, that there shall not be room enough to receive it. And *I will rebuke the devourer for your sakes, and he shall not destroy the fruits of your ground.*"

Obviously, then, God protected Mr. Moore's grapes so the birds would not eat them, just as He promised He would.

But how did the birds know that God was protecting those grapes? That's what I wish one of those birds would tell me.

# VICTORY ON THE PILLOW

A few minutes after Dorothy went to her bedroom to get ready for bed, Mother saw her come out, walk without a word through the living room, through the kitchen, and out the back door. Just a minute or two later, she saw the girl come in again, close the back door firmly behind her, and then go straight through the kitchen and living room and into her bedroom without a "Hello" or a "Hi" or even a glance in her mother's direction.

Something strange was going on, Mother was sure, for she had never seen Dorothy behave like this before. She got up from her chair and started for the bedroom to ask a few questions; then she thought better of it and sat down again. Dorothy would probably tell her all about it in her own good time.

As it turned out, Mother found the answer sooner than she had expected. Next morning when she went into Dorothy's bedroom after Dorothy had left for school, she saw a note lying on the pillow. She picked it up and started to read what it said; but as she read, her eyes misted over and her mind seemed to go back to events that had taken place more than six months before.

Back about that time, Dorothy had asked her mother if it wouldn't be all right for her to wear a bracelet. "Some of the other girls at school are getting them," she explained..

"But you know what the Bible says about jewelry, don't you, dear?" Mother said. "You've memorized that text in 1 Timothy 2:9 that says that women should dress modestly, without 'gold, or pearls, or costly array.'"

"But, Mother," Dorothy said, "it's just a bracelet."

"I know, dear," Mother said. "But bracelets are jewelry."

Mother saw a dark scowl come over Dorothy's face, and it hurt her as if a great knife were being cut into her heart. For up to this time Dorothy had always been willing to accept her mother's counsel.

Mother watched as the weeks went by, and she was glad to notice that Dorothy never wore a bracelet. Then after about three months there was a story in a magazine all about jewelry. The magazine was called Guide, and Dorothy got one every week at church. Mother happened to see the story. She read it, and thought it was very good. She asked Dorothy if she had read it.

"Mm-huh," Dorothy nodded.

"What did you think of it?" Mother asked.

"Mmm," Dorothy grunted.

Mother guessed that Dorothy hadn't yet given up the idea of buying a bracelet. She slipped an arm around Dorothy's shoulders and said, "Pray about it, dear."

Dorothy squirmed out from her mother's arm and stalked off angrily.

Mother sighed and determined to pray harder than ever. She did not realize what was going on in Dorothy's mind. She did not know, for instance, that Dorothy had gone out and bought herself a bracelet and was wearing it whenever she was away from the house. Dorothy knew she shouldn't wear it. She knew she ought to get rid of it. But she wanted to wear it so much! She prayed about it. She thought through what the Bible said. It was a tremendous battle, and it went on for six months.

Now Mother, still standing by Dorothy's bed, blinked the mistiness from her eyes and read the note she had found on the pillow.

"Dear Mother: You don't know it, but six months ago I bought a bracelet, and I've been wearing it when you weren't around. I've prayed a lot about it, and at last I've gotten the victory. Last night I took the bracelet outside and threw it in the garbage can. I'll never wear it again. Your loving daughter, Dorothy."

Mother was so happy when she read that, that she dropped a tear right in the middle of the note paper.

I'm wondering if there is some victory you need to win. With Jesus' help, why don't you win that victory today? Then put a little note on your pillow, telling Mother all about it. What a lot of happy mothers there could be tomorrow morning!

## "THESE ARE FOR THE GARBAGE CAN, DAD"

That story about Dorothy reminds me of Jimmy. He was six, and he loved to look at the comics.

One evening he was looking at them (he couldn't read yet) when he called out, "Oh, Daddy! Come look at this! It's real exciting!"

Daddy knelt down beside him on the floor. He always felt sad when he saw Jimmy with the comics and hoped someday he could get him to understand what trash they are.

He looked where Jimmy was pointing. "You see, Daddy, this bad man was going to kill this good one, but the good man pulled his gun out real fast and shot him first. Served him right, didn't it, Daddy!"

Daddy sighed. What should he do?

He said, "Say, it is exciting! How many people did the bad man shoot?"

"Two or three this week," Jimmy said. "But he got lots more last week!"

"I see," said Daddy. "And how about the good man? How many did he shoot?"

"Oh, he always shoots the bad men."

"Very interesting," Daddy said. "But tell me, Jimmy, when Jesus was on earth, did He shoot bad people?"

"No," Jimmy said, not quite sure where Daddy was leading, but feeling a bit suspicious already.

"Then if this man is doing things Jesus wouldn't do, do you think he's a good man to read about?"

"Um, no," Jimmy said, now quite sure he knew what Daddy was getting at.

"If Jesus were to come in here right now and see you reading these comics, would you be happy or ashamed?"

"I'd try to throw them away quick so He wouldn't see," Jimmy said.

"Good for you," Daddy said. "So why not throw them away now?"

"That's what I'm going to do," Jimmy said. And he did.

Jimmy's daddy told me a few weeks ago that he never snatched the comics away from Jimmy when he caught him reading them. He would sit down beside him, instead, and explain what was wrong with them. Once he asked Jimmy how he would feel if his Sabbath School teacher walked in and found him reading them. At other times he would explain that the comics are full of murder and hate and lying and disobedience and unfaithfulness and just plain foolishness—all the things God asks Christians to stay away from.

One day Jimmy asked, "Daddy, aren't there any good comics?"

Daddy searched a long time. Finally he found a little book that looked like comics, but was really about animals. He showed it to Jimmy.

"These comics are all about animals," he said. "If you look at them, you'll learn about the wonderful things God has taught animals to do."

Not long after this, Jimmy's next-door neighbor cleaned out his old comics and brought them over for Jimmy. He piled them up in the kitchen.

Daddy saw them and wanted to throw them out right away, but just then there was something he had to do in the garage.

Time passed quickly while Daddy worked. Mother was taking a nap—or maybe she was shopping, I'm not quite sure. At all events, Jimmy was left to himself for a while. He saw that great pile of comics—and dived right in.

Daddy heard someone calling and looked up. Jimmy was standing in the garage door, his arms full of comics. "These are for the garbage can, Daddy," he said. "Please take the lid off so I can throw them in."

Daddy ran to remove the lid, smiling all over as he came. Jimmy went on to explain what he had done. "I went through those comics in the kitchen, and there were only two or three of those good animal ones. The others are rubbish. Wait a minute and I'll go back for the rest."

Do I need to say anything about us who are older having as much good sense as a six-year-old, when it comes to choosing what we read?

## FIFTEEN ROADS TO CAMP

It was time for family worship again.

Jim flopped into his regular chair. Family worship! He was tired of it!

Father took up the Bible from its usual place, turned to the chapter for the day, and began to read—just as he always did. Jim stirred restlessly.

Father read on. But when he came to the bottom of the page and turned the leaf, he caught sight of Jim's brooding, rebellious face.

"Son!" he exclaimed. "What's the matter?"

"Aw, Dad!" Jim exploded. "Why do we have to sit here every day and listen to that old stuff?"

Barbara was shocked. She was Jim's little sister. "Jim!" she scolded. "How can you talk like that?"

Daddy smiled at her. "It isn't wrong to ask why we should read the Bible, Sis. Jim has asked a very important question, and it deserves a careful answer. Most of the trouble in the world would come to an end overnight if only people knew why they should read the Bible."

Daddy closed the Book, though he kept his finger in the place where he had been reading. There was silence around the family circle as everyone wondered what he was going to say next. Jim felt his anger cool. He wished he hadn't been so emphatic, since Daddy was so willing to answer his objection.

"Son," Dad said at last, "look at it this way. Suppose you wanted to go camping overnight. You packed your equipment, you loaded your bicycle, you set out. After you had gone a mile or two the road divided. How would you know whether to go to the right or to the left?"

Jim thought a moment. "I suppose I'd look for a sign."

"A good answer, Son. But suppose there were two signs, and one sign said that the left-hand road led to the camp and the other sign said that the right-hand road led to the camp, how would you know which road to take then?"

"I wouldn't."

"All right," Daddy went on. "Now suppose that instead of there being two roads for you to choose between there were many more, say ten or fifteen. Suppose they all looked very much alike and that each one had a sign that said, 'This is the way to camp'? What would you do?"

"He'd be confused," Barbara said.

"Sure would," Jim grinned.

"It is time for worship to be over tonight," Dad said, "so I won't try to give you a complete answer now. We'll close our worship with prayer in the usual way; then if you children would like, look up John 14:6 and see what it says. Tomorrow night we'll go on discussing Jim's question."

As soon as he rose from his knees, Jim hurried to find Dad's text. Barbara read it too, with her hand tucked through Jim's arm.

"What's that got to do with fifteen roads to camp?" she asked. "Oh, dear, I can't wait till tomorrow night. I wish Dad had finished what he started."

You can be sure that Jim and Barbara were in their chairs ready for family worship the next evening, even before Mother and Dad came into the living room.

As soon as Father appeared, Barbara said, "Don't forget, Daddy, you have to finish answering Jim's question. We both read John 14:6, but I don't see what it's got to do with why we have to read the Bible—or with fifteen different roads to camp."

Daddy settled down in his chair. "As soon as Mother is comfortable, I will continue."

"I'm comfortable," Mother announced. "And I'm as eager to know what you are going to say as Jim and Barbara are."

"Last night," Daddy began, "Jim asked me, Why do we have to read the Bible? and I asked him how he would find his way to camp if there were fifteen different roads going in fifteen different directions, and each one had a sign saying, 'This is the way to camp.'

"Well, look at it this way. Everyone wants to be happy and successful in life. But just as there is only one road that leads to camp, so there is only one road that leads to success.

"How can a boy or girl growing up know which way to choose? Almost every book on these shelves—" Daddy waved a hand toward the tall bookcase—"almost every book you will ever pick up, tries to tell the reader how to make his life happy and successful. Every book recommends one way or another.

"Brightly colored advertisements tell you that smoking is the sure way to be happy; others say that drinking will make you successful."

"They can't all be right!" Jim interrupted.

Dad nodded and went on. "God is the only One who knows the right road for us to take. Through the ancient prophets He told the people of long ago which road that was. Some of the people were willing to follow it; others chose different roads.

"For instance, Eve decided that the best road to happiness was to eat the forbidden fruit. Moses decided that the best way to success was to commit murder. He killed an Egyptian and buried him in the sand. Samson decided that the only right way to a happy life was to marry a girl who was not converted. Judas was sure that he would be really happy only if he betrayed Jesus.

"They all thought they were choosing the right way. The Bible tells us which road they chose and where that road actually led them.

"You are still young, Jim and Barbara. Many times in your lives you will have to choose which road you will take. Sometimes, Barbara, you will feel absolutely sure that the only way you can be happy is to quarrel with your big brother. Maybe, Jim, you will be sure you just have to boss your little sister."

Jim squirmed but said nothing.

"At school the fellows will tell you that the best way to get good grades is to cheat once in a while, or the best way to be happy is to go out with the boys and smoke, or perhaps to listen to their smutty jokes. All sorts of people will tell you the way they think is right."

"How can you tell who's right?" Barbara asked, a questioning look in her eyes.

Daddy smiled. "Can you repeat the verse I gave you?"

"Sure," Jim said. "We memorized it in church a while ago. 'Jesus saith unto him, I am the way, the truth, and the life.' Hey! I see it now! The only real way to happiness is to live like Jesus. And—and—we have to read the Bible to find out how Jesus lived and how stupid people are when they try to live any other way. Now, why didn't I think of that before!"

Mother reached over and took his hand in hers. "I think, Father," she said, and her tone was unusually serious, "I think our young son will be a man sooner than we expected."

# A LITTLE BIT OF HELP

There were strange things going on in Marsha's church-school classroom. Every so often one of the students would get up and leave. After a few minutes he would come back, nod to someone else, and that person would get up and leave.

But though such activity would have seemed strange to someone visiting the room, it was really very plain and proper to those who understood.

The secret lay in the fact that for several weeks the church pastor had been holding a special Bible class. He had finished the studies a short while before, and had asked the students to tell him if they wished to give their hearts to Christ and be baptized. He had written down the names of all the children who raised their hands, and then he had told them that he would come over and talk to everyone on his list, one by one, in another room. "That way I can answer any questions you may have," he said. "And," he smiled, "I can find out if you know as much about the Bible as a new church member ought to."

Now he was almost through. Marsha looked around to make sure. She knew Jack and Rachel hadn't gone in to visit the pastor, because they were baptized already. And George hadn't gone either, but he wasn't planning to join the church. In fact, he was making fun of the whole thing.

"That leaves only Carol—and me," thought Marsha. "Oh, dear, I didn't hold up my hand the other day, and the pastor won't call for me, and I want to be baptized so much."

She tried to get her mind back onto what the teacher was saying, but the Holy Spirit was talking to her just then, and she had to listen to Him.

And then the teacher said it was time for a break. Marsha went outside with the others, but she looked so sad that Patsy came over and asked her what the trouble was.

"I want to be baptized," Marsha explained. "And I can't be, because I didn't give the pastor my name the other day when he asked us to raise our hands."

"That's easy," said Patsy. "Just go in and tell him." "I can't," said Marsha. "I'm scared."

"Oh, no," scoffed Patsy gently. "Not scared of our pastor! Why, he's nice."

"But I am scared," said Marsha. She looked so worried and sad that Patsy slipped an arm around her to cheer her up.

"Tell you what," Patsy said, brightening. "I'll go in with you. How'll that be? I'll go and ask teacher right now if I can. Then you won't need to be afraid."

"Thank you so much," said Marsha, looking happy for the first time that morning.

That's how it came about that a few minutes later two girls came into the little room where I was interviewing the children who wanted to be baptized. And it explains, too, why Marsha was baptized with the others a few weeks later.

It makes me wonder. Is there a boy or girl in your class who would like to follow Jesus, but is afraid to? Perhaps a little bit of help from you is just the thing he needs.

# THE COURAGE OF THE SERGEANT

At three o'clock on the afternoon of July 3, 1863, the lookouts with the Northern Army stationed at Gettysburg shouted, "The enemy is advancing."

A mile away, fifteen thousand men of Pickett's division stepped out from among the trees and began marching toward the Northern lines. Shoulder to shoulder they came, rank upon rank, line upon line, silently, irresistibly, down the side of the ridge, across the creek at the bottom, up the long, gentle slope to the rock wall that protected the Northern forces.

It was the South's supreme effort. The outcome of the battle, the turn of the war, the destiny of the nation, was tied up in the success or failure of this charge.

The Northern cannon fired on the advancing brigade, and thousands of soldiers fell. But the living came on. And when those valiant men reached the wall, Webb's brigade, stationed at the corner of the wall, fell back. Southern soldiers poured over. If enough of them crossed the wall, they could divide the Northern Army and win the war.

The North had men enough and guns enough to stop them, but at this moment Webb's men were confused and frightened, and so their guns were useless. What was needed right now was just one man with courage to inspire Webb's men with new confidence.

Lieutenant Frank Haskell, a staff officer, coming by on horseback, saw the problem and called to a major, "Major, lead your men over the crest. They will follow."

But the high-ranking officer replied, "By the rule of battle I understand my place is in the rear of the men." Imagine saying that in a time of crisis!

Lieutenant Haskell sneered, "Your pardon, sir; I see your place is in the rear of men."

Then Lieutenant Haskell said to a sergeant, "Sergeant, forward with your color."

The sergeant seized the flag and ran for the enemy's line. At first only one Northerner dared to follow. But the sergeant fell, struck dead by a bullet, and the standard he had courageously carried fell beside him.

The effect was electrical. Webb's men leaped to their feet and fought the enemy, shouting, pushing, firing,. punching. Back the enemy staggered, to the wall, across the wall—and beyond. As suddenly as it had started, the battle was over. The supreme effort of the South had failed.

We are not going to say just now whether the North or the South was in the right. But if you are the minister's son or the banker's daughter, then know that upon you, as upon the major, rests first of all the opportunity to hold high the flag of God's army and lead your classmates in the great battle against the armies of evil.

But if, like that major, you are scared; if you are too tied to your own selfish interests—your TV programs, your fancy clothes, your parties, or whatever; if you are afraid you won't be popular with your classmates if you hold God's standards high—then keep quiet. Go back to the rear where you belong, and let the washerwoman's daughter and the floor scrubber's son take over the leadership you are too fearful to assume.

If you are the son or daughter of someone who is not considered very important, take heart. It was the sergeant that led the army to victory, not the major. It is not important what rank or position you hold. It doesn't matter what kind of job your parents have, or what kind of car they drive. If you see the enemy invading your classroom, if some of the students want to smoke or experiment with pot, if some of them bring sexy pictures to school or tell smutty jokes, if you wish someone would put an end to all these evil things, then you lead the way. Stand up for what you know is right. Someone probably will sneer at you at first. Well, the sergeant was killed, and you won't be! As you hold the standard high, others will rally behind you, and you who were no leader will be the acknowledged champion of all that is good and right and lovely in your classroom.

God give you the courage of the sergeant!

## THE WAIST GUNNER'S SACRIFICE

There were many brave men in World War II.

One of the bravest was a waist gunner on a Flying Fortress bomber. Because of him, Sergeant Cunningham came out of the war alive.

Cunningham was the radio operator on a Flying Fortress based at a field thirty-five miles north of London.

One day in the spring, near the end of the war, Cunningham's crew was ordered into the air with a load of bombs for one of the enemy's great cities.

It was pleasant flying over the English countryside. The flowers were coming out, and the trees were putting on new leaves. The war seemed far away.

Over enemy territory the situation was very different. The air was filled with bursting shells. Through the window Cunningham saw another Flying Fortress get hit in the wing. It began to fall, spinning faster as it fell, and two parachutes followed it down. "Two men escaped," Cunningham whispered. "Only two."

He thought of his mom and dad. They were hoping so much he'd come back to them. He looked around the cockpit. Every man there, he knew, had someone who longed for the day he'd be going home.

Then he glanced back down the fuselage. The waist gunner was bent over his gun, his eyes glued to the window, every muscle tensed, ready to squeeze the trigger the moment an enemy fighter came into range. He was a quiet sort, that waist gunner. Never said very much about himself. But he and Cunningham had had a few chats together. And once the gunner had pulled out his wallet and shown him pictures of his kid brother and sister. He was so proud of them. "Can't wait to see them again," he had said.

There was a crackling in the earphones, and Cunningham had to concentrate on a message coming in. But before the message was half finished, there was a tremendous explosion just outside the plane and a piece of shrapnel pierced the wall and smashed Cunningham's oxygen equipment.

Cunningham knew at once that he was doomed. In minutes he would pass out, and then, unconscious and helpless, he would die from the lack of oxygen at that high altitude. Already he was growing dizzy. He fumbled with the valves. He was falling

He opened his eyes. What had happened? His head ached. Why was he on the floor? What was that hole in the fuselage? Oh, yes, a shell— It had broken his oxygen mask. Then what was this mask on his face? Why was he still able to breathe?

He struggled to get up and look around.

Just a few feet away, his face to the floor, lay the waist gunner. Dead. His oxygen mask was gone.

Sergeant Cunningham was wearing it! The waist gunner had put it on him and then died in his place.

"Greater love hath no man than this, that a man lay down his life for his friends." John 15:13.

Jesus said that years ago. The waist gunner made it real.

# GO BAKE A CAKE!

One day Marje said to me, "I don't want anyone telling me what I have to do. I want to live my life my own way."

She was twenty years old, and should have known better.

"No," she said, "I don't want anyone reading to me out of the Bible or any other good book. I'm tired of listening to that old stuff. I want to live my life my own way. Thank you!"

Well, I couldn't stop her.

But I tried an experiment. I bought a box of cake mix. I gave it to her and said, "Please do me a favor. Make me a cake exactly according to the directions on the back of this box."

She looked at me in a funny way and said, "Are you trying to tell me something?"

"Sure," I said. "I may even use you for a sermon illustration someday—or write a story about you."

She was a good sport, and she made the cake exactly according to the directions. How do you suppose it turned out?

From the way I hear people talking sometimes, that cake should have turned out terribly. "If you do what Mother and Dad tell you," they say, "if you obey the teachers at school, you'll never have any fun in life."

Well, believe it or not, that cake, made exactly according to directions, turned out very well. I ate as much of it as I could get, but everyone else wanted a piece too.

So far the experiment was turning out my way, but I wasn't finished. I said to Marje, "Now that you have made a cake according to the directions, I want you to do the opposite. Go into the kitchen and try to make a cake without following any directions at all."

I knew that wouldn't be hard for Marje, for she is a good cook, and I'm sure she could make a cake from memory.

She gave me that same funny look, and I told her I most certainly was planning to use her for a sermon illustration. She grinned.

A few days later she told me the new cake was finished.

All the way to Marje's house I was thinking of what some teenagers have told me. "You've got to go out and be free if you want a happy life," they say. "You can't be bound down to rules all the time." Well, I was about to see a cake that was not bound down by any rules. It really ought to be wonderful.

It was wonderful. Fearful and wonderful. It was just a bit thicker than a pancake. And tough. If you picked it up by the edge it wobbled slightly.

"Thank you," I said to Marje. "You have given me an absolutely splendid sermon illustration."

If you have this same idea that Marje had—that you ought to be allowed to live your life your own way, and nobody will be allowed to advise you or counsel you—go bake a cake!

Better yet, make two. Make the first according to the rules on the box, then try to make one out of your own imagination. I think your mother will let you.

If you cannot even make a good cake without following directions, how can you possibly make a good life without following directions?

# PIANO-PLAYING RABBIT

Have you heard of the rabbit that can play the piano? He doesn't just run up and down the notes, either. He plays hymns well enough for church.

And that isn't all. He can play baseball. He hasn't hit a home run yet, but doubtless with a little more practice he will be able to do that too.

I happen to know this clever rabbit quite well, for he stays most of the time in my top dresser drawer.

He died some years ago, yet last night I watched him thread a needle and sew on a button!

Stranger still, he couldn't do any of these unusual things until he was dead!

Indeed, if he hadn't died, I suppose he would never have been anything but an ordinary rabbit. He would have gone on hopping around, nibbling carrots and digging holes to live in, just as rabbits do.

But as I said, this rabbit died. He stopped doing the things ordinary rabbits do. It seemed for a while as though the end of all things had come for him. As it turned out, however, his death was just the beginning.

For someone made that rabbit into a glove, a beautiful, fur-lined glove, and the glove was given to me for a birthday present.

The glove couldn't do a thing as it lay in the pretty gift box. But the minute I put my hand into it, that dead-rabbitturned-into-a-glove suddenly came alive. It began to do all sorts of things.

But the things it did now were not the things that living rabbits do. Oh, no. They were much more clever than that. The things it did now were the things I did. That's when I discovered it could play the piano. So long as it was on my hand, it could play as well as I could!

And as time went on I noticed that as it trusted me enough to let me do whatever I wanted with it, that dead rabbit was able to do almost anything a human being could do. Certainly no living rabbit could have done so well.

The reason I tell you all this is that a great many people I know wish they could live the Christian life. They know they are doing many things they shouldn't, and they try hard to do what is right. But they keep on failing till they get discouraged. Some I know have even given up completely and gone out into the world.

Let me tell you the secret of successful Christian living. You have to die first. I know you do, because I read of a man who died, and he was able to do much better things after he died than ever he could before.

His name was Paul. He wrote, "I am crucified with Christ: nevertheless I live; yet not I, but Christ liveth in me: and the life which I now live in the flesh I live by the faith of the Son of God." Galatians 2:20.

What he meant, of course, was that the sinful old life in which he had been unkind and cruel had been put to death.

Now Jesus had come to live in him (like my putting my hand into the glove), and as long as Paul had enough faith in Jesus to let Jesus do anything He wanted with him, Paul did, not the sinful things he used to do, but the good things Christ did.

And if you will put to death your bad habits and sinful thoughts, and ask Jesus to come and live in you, you will soon be doing the good things Jesus would do if He were in your place.

## HOW TO HANDLE DAD

Supper was over. Janet felt her stomach tighten into a knot. She dreaded what was coming next.

Dad looked angrier than usual this evening. His face was dark and sullen as he laid his fork against the edge of his plate. "Well, Mother," he snarled, "are you coming with me tonight, or are you going to your old meeting?"

"Now, John." Mother's voice was high and scolding. "Why do you ask such foolish questions? I have told you again and again that I can't come with you anymore to the places you go. You want to go to a theater tonight, or down into that cheap joint of yours and play pool and gamble with the men and get drunk. Ever since I found Christ at these meetings I have lost all interest in your activities. You know drinking and gambling are wicked. Your mother told you so when you were a boy, and I have told you so. Why don't you stop? I just don't understand how a man with any sense at all can keep on doing something when he knows it is wrong."

When Father answered, Janet noticed that his voice was low and even, and she guessed that he was furiously angry inside. "I hate your new religion," he said. "Before you began going to those meetings at the church, we used to have good times together. Well—" he pushed back from the table— "if you won't come with me, I'll go find me some other woman who will."

He left the house slamming the door behind him. Presently Mrs. McAllister, one of the women from the church, stopped by and took Mother and Janet to the meeting. Father was still out when they returned, and Janet cried herself to sleep. It seemed as though home had become one continual battleground lately, and Mother and Dad were always fighting. Why, she kept asking herself, why would religion have such a bad effect?

Dad was still sullen at breakfast. After he left for work, Janet said, "Mother, there must be a better way. Why don't you go to the preacher and ask him how we ought to handle Dad?"

"I think maybe I will," Mother said. "We surely must think of something. He's going to lose his soul if he keeps on like this."

Janet could hardly wait to get home after school. She ran into the house. To her amazement, the front room was spotlessly clean. "Mother!" she exclaimed. "Are we having company?"

"I cleaned it for your father," Mother said.

"Wha—why, is he sick or something?"

"It's all part of the plan," Mother said, wiping her hands on her apron. "Sit down, and I'll tell you what the preacher said when I visited him this morning."

Janet sat, and Mother began. "I told the preacher all about Dad and the trouble we have been having. He said that of course I shouldn't go with him to theaters and bars and gambling houses. He also said that we shouldn't mention religion to him again. He said, "Live your religion; don't just talk about it. Always have the house tidy when your husband comes home, and make sure you are dressed attractively.' He said that we should lay out Dad's clothes for him so he wouldn't have any trouble dressing before he goes out in the evening."

"Well!" Janet exclaimed. "That surely is different from what we have been doing! Do you suppose maybe I ought to go up and do my bed? Dad always fusses when he finds I haven't made it. He'd probably faint if he saw me make it every morning! But it just might impress him. And maybe I'd better wear a dress for supper instead of those old slacks I usually have on. And how about some flowers for the table? And, say, couldn't we eat in the dining room instead of the kitchen? We'll treat him like a VIP."

Janet was really getting caught up with the new plan for handling Dad. But would it work?

Well, if Dad noticed, when he came home, that the house was spotless and that supper was served in the dining room instead of the kitchen, with a tablecloth on the table, and flowers, he didn't say so.

As supper ended, Mother said, "Father, I'm sorry I've been trying to cram my religion down your throat. I'm not going to mention religion anymore, and if you want to keep going to those places downtown, go right ahead. I won't object. Would you be willing to take me to the church on your way downtown? That way I'd enjoy being with my friends, and you could enjoy being with yours. Then if you picked me up about nine or nine-thirty, I'd spend the rest of the evening with you at home doing the things we like to do together."

Janet clenched her fists under the table and prayed silently as hard as she could. Daddy just had to accept this proposition!

And he did. He said he thought it would be a good arrangement.

Next morning after she woke up, Janet asked Mother how the evening had turned out. "Wonderful, dear," Mother said. "After you were in bed, we went for a short walk." Janet thought for a moment Mother looked as young as the girls at school. There was a faraway look in her eyes.

Mother said, "It was a lovely night. We haven't had a walk like that since we were dating each other back in high school."

Janet hoped, of course, that under the new plan Daddy would soon start coming to church. It didn't work out that way. Daddy seemed as uninterested as ever.

But Janet and Mother made sure that the house was always comfortable when Daddy came home from work. Supper was always treated like a special occasion. They made sure their hair was neatly fixed, and they dressed in something attractive. Janet took it on herself to be sure Father's clothes were always cleaned and ironed and in their right places so he could change into them easily whenever he wanted to. She was particularly careful not to argue. She made it a habit to smile and be cheerful.

Still Father said not one word about going to church. Three weeks passed.

Then one morning, just before Janet left for school, Mother told her, "Last night Daddy said, "I'm not going to try to find another woman to marry. There couldn't be any other woman in all the world who would take such good care of me."

Janet was so thrilled she threw her arms around Mother's neck. But the school bus came just then and she had to run.

Five weeks went by. Supper was over. Janet was relaxed. She no longer feared angry outbursts from her father. But she was anxious, nevertheless. For the meetings at the church were nearly over, and she had hoped so very much that Father would attend some of them. If he didn't start soon it would be too late.

Father pushed back from the table. "Mother," he said, "about those meetings you've been going to. Do you think that maybe I could go with you tonight? I want to find out what it is you are learning that makes you and Janet so nice to me."

Several months have passed since that wonderful night. Janet's father is now a member of the church. Janet's home is happier than it ever was before. And if your home isn't as happy as you would like it to be, handle your dad the way Janet handled hers. Certainly it's worth a try.

# KINDEST MAN WHO EVER LIVED

The kindest man who ever lived was born many years ago.

Once he went to a wedding. Afterward, during the reception, when the refreshments were being served, there were so many more guests than had been expected, that the supply of grape juice ran low. This kind man knew that the hostess would be embarrassed, so quietly he told the servers to fill several large pitchers with water. When they took the water out of the pitchers, it was grape juice! How thrilled the hostess was when she saw it! You can read the whole story in the second chapter of the book of John.

The man's name, of course, was Jesus. How He did enjoy making people happy!

One day, not long after the wedding, a rich man came to Him and said that his son was ill. Jesus told him, "Go on home. Your son will live." When the man arrived home, he found his son already well. And when the father began asking questions, he discovered that it was at the very time Jesus had talked to him that his son had begun to get better. You can read that story in John 4:46–53.

Children loved to be near Him. They climbed into His lap or sat around on the grass and listened for hours while He told them stories—and how He did love to talk to them!

The older people liked to listen to Him too. One day more than five thousand came to hear Him speak near the lake of Galilee. What He said was so interesting and helpful that no one seemed to notice how fast time was passing. The crowd even forgot about lunch, too, till Jesus stopped talking late in the afternoon. Then they suddenly realized how hungry they were.

Jesus might have said to them, "Hurry on home and have a good supper." But He knew they would be happier if they could eat right then. So when a boy offered Him his lunch of five buns and two fish, Jesus accepted it. He broke it in his hands and fed the whole multitude. See John 6:1–14.

One day when Jesus was preaching in the synagogue, He saw a man whose hand was withered. He stopped preaching and said to the man, "Stand up."

Then, while everyone was watching he told the man to stretch out his withered hand—and the man did it! His hand was cured just that quick, and the man told everyone he met for years afterward about the wonderful thing Jesus had done for him. See Mark 3:1–5.

So it was wherever Jesus went. He cheered up the discouraged, comforted the sad, fed the hungry, and clothed the poor.

You would think everyone would have loved Him. But they didn't. Cruel men arrested Him. They stripped the clothes from His back and whipped Him. They accused Him of many things He had never done. And then they crucified Him. They drove nails through His hands and His feet, and stood around laughing at Him while He died.

But after He died, Jesus came to life again, and He's living in heaven today, still the kindest Man who ever lived. He wants to be kind to you.

If you're in trouble, ask Him to help you, and He will. If you need assistance with your studying, He'll help make it easier. If you have bad habits you need to overcome, He'll help with those too.

And if someday you want to thank Him for being so kind, just bow your head and say, "Thank You, Jesus, for being so good to me."

# JESUS IS COMING SOON!

One of the things Jesus liked to talk about the most while He was on earth was His second coming. Especially as He came near to the time when He would be crucified, He talked more and more about when He would be coming back in great power and glory. Perhaps it helped keep Him from thinking too much about the pain and agony He would have to endure on the cross.

On the last Thursday evening, while Jesus was walking to the Garden of Gethsemane just before He was arrested, the disciples were very sad. Jesus said to them, "Let not your heart be troubled: ye believe in God, believe also in Me." John 14:1. Jesus was the One who was about to be crucified, yet He tried to encourage the disciples. They should have been encouraging Him instead, shouldn't they? They were sure that if Jesus died they would never see Him again, but He knew better.

"In My Father's house are many mansions," He told them. "I go to prepare a place for you. And if I go and prepare a place for you, I will come again, and receive you unto Myself; that where I am, there ye may be also."

Jesus was very plain about it. "I will come again." But the disciples didn't understand, and they still felt sad.

Six weeks later, after Jesus had been crucified and had risen from the dead, He led the disciples to the top of the Mount of

Olives beside Jerusalem. While He was talking to them and telling them what they should do, they were amazed to see Him slowly rising from the earth. They saw Him go higher and higher until a cloud of angels surrounded Him and they could not see Him anymore.

While they were still gazing upward for one last glimpse, they heard a voice say, "Ye men of Galilee, why stand ye gazing up into heaven?"

They turned to see who was talking and were surprised to find two men dressed in white clothes. These men said, "This same Jesus, which is taken up from you into heaven, shall so come in like manner as ye have seen Him go into heaven." Acts 1:11.

This time the disciples understood. Cheerfully they hurried back to Jerusalem. Ten days later they preached such tremendously effective sermons that three thousand people were converted in one day! The rest of their lives they devoted their time to telling everyone they could that Jesus would be coming back.

Paul was not one of the disciples, but when he learned that Jesus planned to return to the earth, he traveled thousands of miles preaching the wonderful news. He called Christ's coming the "blessed hope" (Titus 2:13), and in a letter he wrote to the church members in Thessalonica, he described how Jesus would come.

He told them, "The Lord Himself shall descend from heaven with a shout, with the voice of the Archangel, and with the trump of God." What an exciting event it will be!

Then he added something that has made people happy ever since. "The dead in Christ shall rise first: then we which are alive and remain shall be caught up together with them in the clouds, to meet the Lord in the air: and so shall we ever be with the Lord." 1 Thessalonians 4:16, 17.

When John was an old man, he was banished to the Isle of Patmos. He also looked forward to the day when Jesus would come back. He wrote, "Behold, He cometh with clouds; and every eye shall see Him." Revelation 1:7.

There can be no doubt at all that Jesus is coming back to earth again. We even know what His coming will be like.

But when will He come? We'd all like to know that, wouldn't we? The disciples were curious about it too. One afternoon they were sitting with Jesus on the Mount of Olives, having a long talk with Him, when one of them said, "Tell us, . . . what shall be the sign of Thy coming, and of the end of the world?" Matthew 24:3.

Jesus gave them several signs. You can read about them in Matthew 24.

Perhaps the most important sign he gave them that afternoon was, "This gospel of the kingdom shall be preached in all the world for a witness unto all nations; and then shall the end come." Verse 14.

When Jesus gave that sign, hardly anyone knew about Him—only the disciples and a few thousand people living nearby.

How different it is today! Everywhere you travel around the world you can find Christian churches with ministers preaching the gospel of Christ's kingdom. Jesus said that when the gospel was being preached in all the world, then the end would come. So His coming can't be far away.

Another important sign that tells us when Jesus is coming is found in Daniel 12:4. Daniel wrote that in "the time of the end: many shall run to and fro, and knowledge shall be increased."

Did ever people run to and fro as much as they do nowadays? They aren't even content with millions of cars, or with airplanes that fly faster than sound, but now they have even gone out to the moon and back and talk of flying to Mars. Nothing like this was ever seen on earth before. Surely we are living in the time of the end.

And what about the increase of knowledge? Scientists tell us that they are doubling our knowledge of the world every four or five years. Libraries aren't big enough to hold all the new things people are finding out. Children in grade school these days are being taught things that even college professors did not know ten years ago!

We are all aware, though we don't like to think about it, that there are enough hydrogen bombs to destroy the whole world in fifteen minutes or less. It could happen today—this afternoon. Just that soon! Yet we know the world is not going to be destroyed by hydrogen bombs. Jesus will come before that happens. So His coming can't be far off, can it?

All of this means that soon—during your lifetime—you will look up and see a cloud drawing closer and closer to the earth. As it comes near, you will see that it is full of angels, and Jesus is sitting on a throne in the midst. Then "the kings of the earth, and the great men, and the rich men, and the chief captains, and the mighty men, and every bondman, and every free man" will hide "themselves in the dens and in the rocks of the mountains"; they will call to the rocks and mountains, "Fall on us, and hide us from the face of Him that sitteth on the throne…: for the great day of His wrath is come; and who shall be able to stand?" Revelation 6:15–17.

Who indeed? Only those who have already asked Jesus to forgive their sins and who have been trying by His grace to live a Christian life.

For a moment all will be quiet while even the good people tremble. They always believed that Jesus was great and powerful, but they had never realized He was so mighty as this.

Then, in the silence, comes the clear voice of Jesus calling the dead to wake up. All over the earth graves will open and everyone who died loving Jesus will come forth, alive and well and strong.

Then Jesus will "send His angels with a great sound of a trumpet, and they shall gather together" all the good people "from one end of heaven to the other." Matthew 24:31.

If you give your heart to Jesus and sincerely try to live the way He wants you to, one of those angels will come to you and take you up with all the others to meet Jesus on the cloud.

What a day that will be!

And it won't be long now. Jesus is coming soon!

## ARE YOU READY?

Suppose someone were to come running up to you right now and say, "It's the end of the world!" How would you feel?

One girl said to me once, "I want Jesus to come, but I wish I knew I was ready."

And this problem, I've noticed, is one that bothers many young people. How can we be sure we are ready for Jesus to come?

The first thing to remember is that Jesus wants to save us.

You may have been told that God is keeping a record of all your sins so that in the judgment He can prove you should be kept out of heaven. Now, it is true He is keeping a record. But He is keeping it so that someday He can point to it and say, "The record proves that this boy or girl gave his life to Me. He asked Me to forgive his sins. He is Mine, and no one can take him from Me. He shall live with Me forever."

We know Jesus wants us in heaven, because He said so many times. He prayed to His Father, "I desire that these...may be with Me where I am." He said to the people in Jericho, "The Son of man is come to seek and to save that which was lost." To the crowds who gathered to hear Him preach He said, "Come to Me, all of you." John 17:24, NEB; Luke 19:10; Matthew 11:28, Goodspeed. Jesus wants to save us.

Another thing to remember is that when we ask God to forgive our sins, He forgives us. He doesn't hold our sins against us anymore. We don't need to be afraid that when Jesus comes He will hold up a long list of the sins we have repented of and tell us we can't go to heaven. He has promised that if we repent and confess, He will be "faithful...to forgive." 1 John 1:9. God keeps His promises. He erases our sins from the record book and forgives them. He says, "I will remember their sin no more." Jeremiah 31:34.

Well, now, if Jesus wants to save you, and if you have asked Him to forgive your sins, your record is clear. Why be worried and fearful about His coming? Look forward to His return with joy. Spend time every day reading about Him in the Bible so that you won't get careless, talk to God often in prayer—and start planning now for the good times you'll have in heaven.

But perhaps you have never given your life to God. You have done things that were wrong and have not asked God to forgive you. In that case you ought to be worried, for the Bible makes it very plain that everyone who has not made things right with God will die when Jesus comes. They will be destroyed, Paul wrote, "with the brightness of His coming."

It may be a struggle to admit you have been doing wrong. You may have to cancel some of your plans. You may have to break habits you cherish. You may have to give up things you enjoy doing. Some young people find this the hardest battle of their lives. They would rather do anything else than come to God and say, "I have been wrong. Please forgive me."

Yet this is the best decision anyone ever made! If you have never surrendered your life to God, do so now. God is calling you. Stop reading for a minute and listen. Think how kind Jesus was to come to earth to die for you. Remember the wonderful things He has promised to do for you in the future. Think how much you will lose if you reject His invitation.

Now bow your head and say, "Dear God, forgive me for my sins Help me to live like Jesus and be ready for Him."

God will hear your prayer—and He will make sure you are ready when Jesus comes.

We invite you to view the complete selection of titles we publish at:
**www.TEACHServices.com**

We encourage you to write us with your thoughts about this, or any other book we publish at:
**info@TEACHServices.com**

TEACH Services' titles may be purchased in bulk quantities for educational, fund-raising, business, or promotional use.
**bulksales@TEACHServices.com**

Finally, if you are interested in seeing your own book in print, please contact us at:
**publishing@TEACHServices.com**

We are happy to review your manuscript at no charge.

www.ingramcontent.com/pod-product-compliance
Lightning Source LLC
LaVergne TN
LVHW020638100826
845148LV00012B/2226

* 9 7 8 1 5 7 2 5 8 5 7 3 7 *